The Expert's Guide to Excellent Wines

The Expert's Guide to Excellent Wines

More than 600 highly-rated wines for $10 or less

COMPILED BY

CLAUDE McGINNIS

Scarborough House

Scarborough House
Lanham, MD 20706

FIRST SCARBOROUGH HOUSE EDITION 1994

Library of Congress Cataloging-in-Publication Data

McGinnis, Claude.
    The expert's guide to excellent
wines : more than 600 highly-rated wines
for $10 or less / compiled by Claude
McGinnis.
        p. cm.
    1. Wine and wine making.   I. Title
TP548.M4684   1994
641.2'2'0296--dc20

ISBN 0-8128-8554-6

Contents

Acknowledgments

Numerous sources were utilized to provide background for this book. These were especially helpful:

The Ashington-Pickett Wine Review
P.O Box 149044
Orlando, FL 32814

Food & Wine Magazine
New York, N.Y. 10036

The Wine Advocate
Parkton, MD 21120

The Wine Enthusiast
Hawthorne, NY 10532

The Wine Spectator
New York, NY 10016

Don Reddick, Wine Supervisor
Harry's Farmers Market
Alpharetta, GA 30076

Especially:

Cary McGinnis Grubb
My faithful computer genius

Introduction

The mystique surrounding wines has persisted for centuries and still intimidates many. Yet it is obvious that some wine tastes better than others. Even the Bible's reference to wine makes it clear that even two thousand years ago people could distinguish one from another - the winemaker does make a difference.

This mystique has discouraged the average wine consumer, the person who just likes to have wine as an aperitif or with a meal. Wines selling for thousands at auctions garner great publicity, and wines generally available for $30.00 or more per bottle tend to discourage the occasional drinker of wine.

And yet there are many wines that sell for $10.00 or less that are excellent examples of that varietal. There is a bewildering amount of information published each year in which various experts rate wines in all price ranges as to quality and taste.

This book is an attempt to condense into usable form the opinion of some of these experts and to put the listings in a logical order for some use, on the spot, by someone interested in less expensive wines. These wines are all rated as being at least "Good." If you were using a scale of 0 to 100, the minimum rating of any wine listed would be 80.

You will find that these wines come from all around the world. The art and science of making wine has become the subject of entire college curricula, and the graduates have spread out and joined with the older winemakers to make excellent wines from what in the past may have been considered ordinary grapes. In Chile, for example, both American and French vintners have purchased large properties and are making very good wines, many of which are listed in the book.

You are urged to explore. Information is included about the compatibility of wines and various foods, but that doesn't preclude you from trying other combinations. Keep in mind that even if you didn't care for a particular wine, you haven't spent very much to try it. Eventually, you may have your own "House Wine," both red and white, but don't let that stop your explorations. Of the more than 600 wines listed, not all of them will be found in your particular location, but there will still be plenty to try.

There are a myriad of grape varieties in the world, more than anyone could possibly list. Some of those wines will be found under the "Red" or White" classification. Don't bypass other sections. Some are sweet, and some are dry. Their characteristics are detailed in the tasting notes.

How To Use This Book

Take this book with you when you shop for wine. The handy size makes it easy to thumb through while standing in front of wine displays. The "Best Buy" designation indicates a special combination of taste, quality, and/or price and is entirely subjective. It does not mean that it will be more appealing to you than another wine on the list, but it is one that will be a good bet to try.

There is also space between the listings to make notes on each wine. Have the book handy when you are "tasting," and write down your impression for future reference.

When you try a new wine, pour a small amount into the glass and swirl it around to bring out the aromas (volatilize the esters). See if you can pick those aromas mentioned in the book - cherry, pineapple, smoke. Then put a little in your mouth and hold it a few seconds before swallowing. Try to pick up the flavors. There is one more; after you swallow, there is an aftertaste - the finish. Each of these can be just a little different. See if you can pick out each one. Jot down your impressions in the book. Make it a tasting book.

David O'Neal was born on November 12th in French Camp, California shortly after World War II. He grew up in Tennessee, Florida and finally back in California. After high school he joined the United States Marine Corps where he received a Presidential Appointment to the US Naval Academy but did not attend. Serving in the war in South Vietnam was his last duty assignment in the Marines.

He has education in City and Regional Planning with graduate studies in Cybernetic Systems. For over ten years he worked as a Business and Computer Systems Consultant. His first book was a technical reference manual published in 1992. *The Pact with Bruno* is the second of three planned novels detailing the life challenges and personal choices of Doug Carlson.

Dave currently resides in the San Francisco Bay Area with his wife, Cheryl. He also has an adult daughter with two grandchildren living several hours away.

Barbera

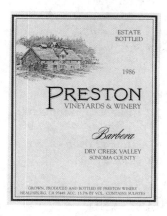

An Italian varietal that seems to have originated in the Astigiano. The grape is grown widely in the Piedmont, Allessandria, Cuneo, and Turin. Barberas are high in tannins when young, but age well. The better ones can easily stand six to eight years in the cellar. Genuine Barbera d'Asti, if correctly cellared for three to four years is truly delicious with softer tannins and bold fruitiness.

CASTELLO DEL POGGIO
1989 Barbera d'Asti
**   Best-now $8-10
Zesty, dry; good berry flavors

DESSILANI
1990 Barbera
**   **Best-now**   **$7-9**
Ripe and mellow; berry, tobacco and oak; uncomplicated

MONTE VOLPE
1991 Barbera Mendocino
***   **Best-93-95**   **$7-9**
Penetrating; fruit, cherry, and berry tastes; brisk

SEBASTIANI
1989 Barbera Sonoma County
**   **Best-now**   **$9-11**
Lively, dry, uncomplicated; fragrant and refreshing

WESTWOOD
1991 Barbera El Dorado Ritchie Vineyard
**   **Best-now**   **$6-8**
Berry tastes; spice overtones; lean on flavor

Beaujolais

About 100 miles south of Burgundy, the chalky limestone hills give way to the granite of the Massif Central. This is where the Gamay grape is grown from which all Beaujolais is made. Unlike the other wine regions of France, the soil here is granitic rather than chalky. The Gamay grape, rejected everywhere else, thrives on this granite soil.

There are three divisions in Beaujolais: Beaujolais Nouveau, Beaujolais Villages, and the ten Beaujolais crus. Beaujolais Nouveau is released, by law, on the third Thursday in November, when it is barely out of the fermentation vats. It is short lived, lasting only three to four months, but it is zesty and fruity.

Beaujolais Villages is a better wine from thirty nine designated Communes. It is deeper in character, more robust, and it should be drunk within a year, no longer.

The ten designated Beaujolais crus are located at the northern end of the region. These wines are luscious, firmer, and longer lasting. Some can be cellared for up to five years. All Beaujolais can be served chilled.

GEORGES DUBOEUF *BEST BUY*
1992 Beaujolais Villages Flower Label
***   **Best-now**   **$5-7**
Rich fruit aromas; mature flavors; silky and sound

GEORGES DUBOEUF *BEST BUY*
1992 Morgon Jean Descombes
***** Best-now   **$8-10**
Lush fruit aromas; focused, silky, and supple

GEORGES DUBOEUF *BEST BUY*
1992 Moulin A Vent Domaine des Rosiers
***** Best-93-95 $9-11
Focused berry and currant scents and flavors; distinctive and full-bodied

GEORGES DUBOEUF   *Best Buy*

1992   Regnie Domaine du Potet
****   Best-now $7-9

Lush, mature berry and fruit harmonized with good acidity; pure pleasure

GEORGES DUBOEUF   *Best Buy*

**1992 Villages Domaine
Granite Bleu**
****   Best-now $6-8

Focused cherry and cassis; mellow fruit; harmonious, mature finish

BARTON & GUESTIER

"Saint Louis" 1991
**   Best-now $6-7

Classic fruity grape; considerable depth for simple Beaujolais; balanced.

BERINGER

1992 Gamay Beaujolais-Nouveau
***   Best-now $5-7

Good fruit; delicate texture; straightforward

DOMAINE CHEYSSON
1991 Chirroubles
***   Best-now $9-11

Focused floral and berry aromas; smooth, rich fruit flavors

GEORGES DUBOEUF
1992 Beaujolais Villages Chateau Des Vierres
***   Best-now $7-9

Fragrant, fruity, mature; silky texture; voluptuous

GEORGES DUBOEUF
1992 Brouilly Chateau des Nerves
***   Best-now $7-9

Firm and ripe; opulent and full-bodied

GEORGES DUBOEUF
1992 Chenas Domaine Des Darroux
***   Best-now $7-9

Lush fruit and spice; sturdy texture; earthy and spicy

GEORGES DUBOEUF
   1992 Fleurie Chateau De Duits
   ***   Best-93-98 $7-9
   *Voluptuous, mature fruit; full-bodied
   and delicious*

GEORGES DUBOEUF
   1991 Fleurie Domaine
   Quatre Vents
   ****   Best-94-98 $8-10
   *Exhuberant fruit; mature and
   flavorful; delicious finish*

GEORGES DUBOEUF
   1992 Julienas Flower Label
   ***   Best-now $7-9
   Sturdy fruit; mature, brisk, and light

GEORGES DUBOEUF
   1992 Morgon Flower Label
   ****   Best-now $7-9
   *Mellow berry fruits; silky, mature;
   mellow finish*

GEORGES DUBOEUF
　　1991 Moulin A Vent Domaine
　　Moulin A Vent
　　***** Best-93-98 $9-11**
　　Mature, ripe fruit flavors; scents of
　　cassis and spice; even texture and
　　flavor

GEORGES DUBOEUF
　　1991 Moulin A Vent Domaine Tour
　　Du Bief
　　***** Best-now $9-11**
　　Firm and focused; generous fruit and
　　oak; gentle tannins

GEORGES DUBOEUF
　　1991 Moulin A Vent Oak Aged
　　***** Best-now $9-11**
　　Lush and spicy; profound fruit tastes;
　　mature and sweet

GEORGES DUBOEUF
1992 Regnie Flower Label
**** Best-now   9-11
Intense berry and cherry aromas and flavors; smooth and tasty

JAFFELIN
1991 Beaujolais Villages Domaine de Riberolles
**** Best-now $7-9
Classic gamay; focused floral scents; fruity flavors

MONTEREY VINEYARDS
1991 Gamay Beaujolais
***   Best-now $5-7
Mouthfilling, fruity; delightfully flavorful

Bordeaux

This is one of the regions in France that produces some of the most famous and expensive wines in the world. In recent years, a number of great vintage years have been recorded: 1986, 1988, 1989, and 1990. Many of these great wines will not be ready to drink for 15 to 20 years. Almost all are a blend of Cabernet Sauvignon, Cabernet Franc, and Merlot. Many of these wines listed can be cellared for two years or more, and they will become softer as the tannins subside. Serve with strong cheeses like bleu, stilton, and goat and serve with duck, beef, and lamb.

MARQUIS DE CHASSE *Best Buy*
   1990 Bordeaux
   **   Best-95-98 $6-8
   Intense, rich, spice and plum tastes

BARTON AND GUESTIER
   1990 Bordeaux Foundation 1725
   **   Best-94-96 $8-10
   Sturdy, tasty; some spice and cherry scents

BARTON AND GUESTIER
   1991 Bordeaux Foundation 1725
   **   Best-now $8-10
   Herbal aromas; fruit and mineral flavors; tasteful

CHATEAU BONNET
   1990 Bordeaux
   **   Best-93-96 $6-8
   Mature fruit; good tannins; pleasant

CHATEAU BONNET
1989 Bordeaux en Futs de Chene Reserve
***   Best-94-95 $9-11
Sound, harmonious currant and cherry tastes

CHATEAU DE LA CLOSIERE
1992   Bordeaux Blanc
***   Best-now $6-8
Robust and mature; conentrated fruit flavors through to the finish

CHATEAU DUCLA
1988 Cuvee Extreme
***   Best-93-95 $9-12
Solid feel, harmonious with some tobacco and cherry taste

CHATEAU LA GABORIE
1989 Bordeaux
**   Best-now $7-9
Rich, round, dark ruby with concentrated fruit

CHATEAU LA MAZEROLLE
1990 Bordeaux
***   Best-96-98 $8-10
*Delicate, dry, butter and cherry
scents and flavors; balanced*

CHATEAU LA TONNELLE
1990 Premieres Cotes de Blaye
**   Best-now $7-9
*Uncomplicated, delicate; cherry and
herb tastes on the palate*

CHATEAU LAROSE
1989 Trintaudon Haut-Medoc
***   Best-now $9-11
*Big berry flavors of Bordeaux;
chocolate undertones; earthy finish*

CHATEAU PITRAY
1990 Cotes de Castillion
**   Best-94-96 $8-10
*Earthy, uncomplicated; fruity, and
zesty*

COUCHEROY
1991 Graves White
***   Best-now $8-11

*Agreeable fruit and citrus aromas
and flavors; brisk with a little flint
taste*

MAITRE D'ESTOURNEL
1989 Boudeaux Rouge
***   Best-now $7-9

*Spicy, earthy berry flavors; light
body; considerable depth*

MICHEL LYNCH
1988 Bordeaux Rouge
**   Best-now $5-7

*Well-made, clean, nice flavors; good
fruit, acid balance*

MOUTON-CADET
1989 Bordeaux
***   Best-94-96 $7-9

*Full-bodied; intense blackberry and
vanilla to savor in a delicious red*

Cabernet Sauvignon

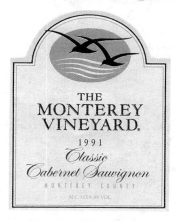

Cabernet Sauvignon has truly found a home in California where it may be the principal great wine. Now in recent years, both Argentina and Chile have begun sending good Cabernets to the United States and both American and French vintners have purchased substantial vineyards there. The wines produced from this grape are dark, rich red. Tasting notes may refer to a huge array of flavors: cherry, berry, cedar, tobacco, peppers, and currants, depending on the vintner and the vintner's style. Some with good tannins will need a few years of aging to mellow. This is a red meat wine, serve with hamburgers, lamb, meat stews, and beef.

CANEPA *BEST BUY*
1991 Maipo Valley
** **Best-now** $5-7
Mature fruit, herb, and cherry;
harmonious blend with nice tannins

GLEN ELLEN *BEST BUY*
1989 California Proprietor's
Reserve
*** **Best-now** $5-8
Plenty of berry and fruit; zesty and
luscious

KOALA RIDGE *BEST BUY*
1990 Barossa Valley
*** **Best-95-97** $8-10
Full-bodied and balanced; piquant
cherry nuances

MONTEREYVINEYARD *BESTBUY*
1990 Monterey County Classic
** **Best-96-95** $5-7
Stout, flavorful herbs; fruity scents
and tastes

TAFT STREET   *BEST BUY*
1991 Sonoma County
***   Best-94-96 $7-9
Fruity scents and flavors; tasty and sound

4 PORTAL DEL ALTO
1990 Maipo Valley
***   Best-93-95 $3-5
Harmonious, even texture; cherry and plum tastes

ARROWFIELD
1990 Cabernet Merlot Australia
***   Best-now $9-11
Spice and berry accents; uncomplicated and smooth

BANDIERA
1989 Napa Valley
***   Best-94-96 $6-8
A luscious, harmonious blend of sturdy cherry, fruit, and oak

BEL ARBORS
1990 California
**   Best-now $5-8
Direct; fruit flavors; refreshing

BODEGAS SAN TELMO
1985 Mendoza
**   Best-now $9-11
Sturdy, spicy, harmonious, and uncomplicated

BODEGAS SAN TELMO
1987 Mendoza Cuesta Madero
**   Best-now $3-6
Ripe, harmonious, and even; fruity and zesty

BON MARCHE
1991 Sonoma County
***   Best-93-95 $6-8
Brisk, rich, fruit, and berry scents and tastes

CALITERRA
1990 Maipo
***   **Best-now**   **$4-7**

Firm, fruity flavors; uncomplicated but zesty taste

CALITERRA
1991 Maipo
**   **Best-now**   **$5-7**

Brisk, uncomplicated, tasty; good currant and cherry flavors

CALITERRA
1988 Maipo Reserva
****   **Best-94-96**   **$8-11**

Mellow, cherry and cedar scents and tastes; full-bodied

CALITERRA
1988 Maipo Reserve
***   **Best-94-96**   **$9-11**

Concentrated cedar and cherry scents and tastes; good tannins

CALITERRA
1989 Maipo Valley
*** **Best-now** $5-8
Licorice undertones; intense berry flavors; long on the finish

CALITERRA
1990 Maipo Valley
*** **Best-now** $5-7
Essence of cedar and generous mature fruit and cherry tastes; uncomplicated

CALLAWAY
1989 California
** **Best-now** $8-10
Tannic, luscious, brisk; uncomplicated

CARA VIEJA
1990 Maule Valley
** **Best-now** 4-6
Sound fruit and berry scents and tastes; uncomplicated

CAVAS LACERNOYA
1988 Penedes
***   Best-94-98 $9-12
Solid, focused; luscious tobacco and cherry scents

CEDAR CREEK
1990 Southeastern Australia Bin 99
**   Best-now $5-7
Berry tastes along with tangy fruit

CHESTNUT HILL
1990 California Coastal Cuvee
***   Best-now $7-9
Intense cherry, oak, and some spice; very palatable

CHRISTIAN BROTHERS
1987   Napa Valley
**   Best-now $7-9
Evocative scents of black cherry, cassis and dry herbs; supple texture; silken finish and great balance; remarkable

COCKATOO RIDGE
1990 Cabernet Merlot South Eastern Australia
**   **Best-now**   **$6-8**
Mature taste; dark side of fruit flavors; luscious

CONCHA Y TORO
1989 Maipo
**   **Best-now**   **$5-7**
Brisk, agreeable currant and berry scents and tastes; straight-forward

CONCHA Y TORO
1988 Maipo Casillero del Diablo Pirque Vineyard Special Reserve
**   **Best-94-96**   **$8-9**
Good herb, cedar, and currant scents and tastes; sound, tasty

CONCHA Y TORO
**1988 Maipo Prique Vineyard
Casillero del Diablo Special Reserve**
** **** Best-now $8-10**
*Delicious herb, cedar, and currant
scents and tastes; sound*

COOK'S
1988 California Captain's Reserve
** Best-now $4-7
Straight-forward; lots of berry flavors

CORBETT CANYON
1989 Alexander Valley Reserve
*** Best-93-94 $8-10
*Concentrated cherry, spice and
currant tastes; full-bodied and even*

COTES DE SONOMA
1990 Sonoma County
** Best-now $6-8
*Supple fruit and spice; pleasant
tannins and oak*

COUSINO-MACUL
1988 Antiguas Reservas
Maipo Chile
***   Best-now $7-9

Enjoyable now but ages very well

DE MARTINO
1990 Maipo Valley
Santa Ines Vineyard
***   Best 94-96 $4-6

*Sound, focused, spice and plum taste;
firm texture*

DOMAINE RABAT
1991 Maipo Valley
**   Best-now $4-6

*Very palatable; cherry and currant
scents and tastes blend with oak*

ERNEST & JULIO GALLO
1986   Sonoma
***   Best-93-96 $4-6

Sturdy, flavorful herbs; good tannins

ERRAZURIZ
1990 Aconcagua Valley Don Maximiano Estate Reserva
**** Best-94-95 $8-9

Opulent fruit, cherry, and currant flavors with the oak; flavorful and lively

FETZER
1990 California Valley Oaks
** Best-now $6-9

Focused; some fruity tastes; round and tasty

GUNDLACH BUNDSCHU
1990 Bearitage Sonoma Valley
** Best-now $9-11

Fragrant and firm; lots of berry and herbs to taste

HAYWOOD
1990 California Vintner's Select
** Best-now $7-9

Tasty, well-balanced, plummy, and zesty

J. LOHR
1989 California Cypress
**   Best-now $6-9

Mature, silky blend with oak over-tones

J. LOHR ESTATES
1988 "Seven Oaks" Paso Robles
**   Best-now $9-11

Ripe cherry flavors; easy, nicely-rounded texture

LA JOTA
NV   Napa Valley Little J
**   Best-now $8-9

Luscious grape scents and tastes; brisk, full-bodied

LAUREL GLEN
1989 Sonoma County Terra Rosa
***   Best   97-98 $8-10

Harmonious blend of berry and currant tastes; refreshing

MCGUIGAN BROTHERS
1992   Australia Bin 4000
**   Best-now $8-10

Rich, fruity; lots of berry scents and tastes

MESSINA HOF
1989 Texas Barrel Reserve
***   Best-95-96 $9-11

Clear, woody, and zesty to savor

MONTEREY VINEYARDS
1991 Classic
***   Best-now $5-7

Solid structure; berry and spice aromas and flavors

MONTEVINA
1990 California
** Best-now $8-10
Even, uncomplicated; some fruit and herbal notes

PHILLIPE-LORRAINE
1989 Napa Valley
*** Best-now 9-11
Tasty, harmonious, fruity, and zesty

RAIMAT
1989 Costers del Segre
** Best-now $7-9
Intense herbal and fruit tastes; big

ROBERT MONDAVI
   1990 California Woodbridge
   **   Best-now $7-9
   Uncomplicated; straightforward;
   some cherry and berry tastes

ROO'S LEAP
   1990 McLaren Vale
   **   Best-now $9-11
   Zesty, fruity, straight-forward,
   flavorful

ROSEMOUNT
   1991 South Eastern Australia
   ***   Best-93-94 $8-11
   Sound, fruity, clean, and zesty

ROUND HILL
   1989 California
   **   Best-now $5-7
   Uncomplicated cherry and berry
   scents and tastes; refreshing

SANTA CAROLINA
1989 Maipo Valley
**   Best-now $7-8

Floral scents; fruit flavors; soft and drinkable now

SANTA RITA
1988 Maipo Valley "120" Label
***   Best-now $5-7

Big, jammy-rich cabernet and berry flavors; soft, some complexity

SANTA RITA
1989 Maipo Valley "120" Label
***   Best-93-96 $6-8

Generous herb, cherry and currant flavors; full-bodied

SEBASTIANI
1991 Sonoma County
***   Best-now $8-11

Citrus blends with dry fruit flavors; very tasty

ST MORILLON
1987 Maipo
** **Best-now** **$5-7**
Plain and zesty cherry tang; very pleasant

STEVENOT
1989 Calaveras County Reserve
** **Best-now** **$9-11**
Slightly acidic; uncomplicated; some fruit flavors

TRENTADUE
1987 Sonoma
*** **Best-now** **$9-11**
Firm, cherry, smoke, and herbs; luscious, mouthfilling

VILLA MT EDEN
1990 California Cellar Select
** **Best-95-97** **$9-11**
Sound touches of currants, plum, and tannin

VILLA MT EDEN
1989 California Cellars Select
***　　Best-96-03　$9-11
Taut, clean, harmonious oak and herbs tastes

VILLA MT. EDEN
1988 California Cellar Select
***　　Best-94-96　$7-9
Brisk, tasty fruit; good tannins

WYNDHAM
1988 South Eastern Autralia Bin 444
**　　Best-now　$6-9
Intense; coarse but good tannins; mouthfilling

Chardonnay

BEAUFORT.

NAPA VALLEY
CHARDONNAY

ALC. 13.5% BY VOL.

The grape vinified in a myriad of styles both in France as well as California, Australia, Argentina, Italy, and Chile. This is the grape used to make Chablis in France (the real thing), as well as Montrachet, Pouilly-Fuisse, and Champagne. Elsewhere, the grape is used to make wine in styles that range from near sweet to dry, some with oak, others with too much oak, some with none at all. Most are aged in stainless steel tanks. Aromas are fruity, sometimes citrusy, spicy, and herbal. This category is worth serious exploration, as you will find all sorts of styles and tastes. You will find favorites that suit different occasions. Chardonnay usually goes well with lighter cheeses, pâtés, chicken, and fish.

CALLAWAY *BEST BUY*
1990 Temecula Calla-Lees
**** Best-93-95 $7-9
Robust and zesty; lots of fruit flavors

GLEN ELLEN *BEST BUY*
1991 California Proprietor's Reserve
*** Best-now $5-8
A little sweet but flavorful; fruity and clean

GRANT SMITH *BEST BUY*
1991 Riverina Valley Vintage Reserve Bin 98
**** Best-now $7-9
Tropical fruit flavors; excellent balance; great flavor

HARDY'S *BEST BUY*
1991 South Eastern Australia Bird Series
*** Best-now $6-9
Fragrant, clean, fruity, and well-balanced

JEAN-CLAUDE BOISSET *BEST BUY*
   1991 Bourgogne Charles de France
   ***   **Best-now**   **$8-10**
   Fruity tastes; toasty and oaky;
   delicious

LABOURE-ROI   *BEST BUY*
   1989 Vin de Pays d'Oc
   **   **Best-now**   **$5-7**
   Zesty, refreshing

SUTTER HOME   *BEST BUY*
   1090   **California Chardonnay**
   **   **Best-now**   **$5-8**
   Exotic flavors, possibly enhanced
   with chenin blanc; fruity, balanced

Payless @ $6.99/ea

WENTE BROS   *BEST BUY*
   1991 Central Coast Estate Grown
   ****   **Best-now**   **$7-9**
   Distinctive; superb tastes of fruit in a
   smooth wine

ALDERBROOK
1989 Dry Creek Valley
** Best-now $6-8

A touch of oak; lightly buttery with a clean, dry finish

ALDERBROOK
1990 Dry Creek Valley
** Best-now $9-11

Robust, concentrated fruit tastes

ANDREW GARRETT
1991 Australia Barrel Fermented
*** Best-93-94 $9-11

Exotic fruits all the way through in a creamy, full-bodied wine

ARCIERO
1990 Paso Robles
* Best-now $7-9

A clean finish; a delicate blend of fruit flavors to start

ARCIERO
1991 Paso Robles
***   Best-93-96 $7-9
Apple and spice; mature and harmo-nious; very flavorful

BABICH
1991 Hawke's Bay
****   Best-95-97 $9-11
Concentrated citrus and exotic fruit; mature, hearty

BANDIERA
1990 Napa County
**   Best-now $5-8
Uncomplicated; lots of fruit and spice aromas and flavors

BARON HERZOG
1990 California Selection
**   Best-now $7-9
Flavorful, zesty, fruit tastes; smooth

BARRIER REEF
1992   South Australia
***   Best-now $6-8**
Concentrated fruit; zesty and pen-
etrating to the finish

BARTON AND GUESTIER
1991 Macon St Louis
**   Best-now $7-9**
Clean, smooth, citrus and apple
scents and tastes

BEAUCANON
1990 Napa Valley
**   Best-now $8-10**
Harmonious blend of citrus and
vanilla flavors; delightful

BEAUCANON
1991 Napa Valley
**   Best-now $9-11**
Zesty, fruit and spice scents and
tastes; a little tart

BEAULIEU
1990 Napa Valley Beaufort
**   Best-now $8-10

Sturdy, tasty combination of fruit and citrus

BEAULIEU
1990 Napa Valley Beautour
**   Best-now $6-9

Fragrant; clean with good fruity and flowery scents

BELVEDERE
1990 Alexander Valley
**   Best-now $7-9

Strong pear and oak tones; uncomplicated

BERINGER
1991 Napa Valley Proprietor Grown
***   Best-now $9-12

Smooth, refreshing, zesty and fruity tastes

BLACK OPAL
1991 South Eastern Australia
*** Best-93-95 $8-10
Creamy butter and fruit; silky texture;
delightful

BON MARCHE
1991 Sonoma County
*** Best-93-94 $7-9
Light, zesty, clean apple scents and
taste

BRUTOCAO
1988 Mendocino
** Best-now $9-11
Hearty, luscious, zesty; some citrus at
the finish

CALITERRA
1992 Curico
** Best-now $6-8
Lots of apple on the nose; brisk,
fresh, uncomplicated

CANTERBURY ·
1990 California
**   Best-now $7-9

*Hearty and smooth; fruit and spice
tones*

CAPE SELECTION
1991Robertson
**   Best-now $6-8

*Uncomplicated fruit and herbal
tastes; brisk, clean*

CASTORO
1990 San Luis Obispo County
**   Best-now $8-10

*Tasty melon and fruit;
uncomplicated, fresh, and clean*

CAVE DE CHARDONNAY
1991 Macon Chardonnay de Chardonnay
**   Best-now $9-11

*Flavorful; austere fruity tastes and
scents*

CHANTEFLEUR
1991 Pays d'Oc
** Best-now $4-6

Tropical fruit flavors; some oakiness; crisp, light, and balanced

CHARLES KRUG
1989 Napa Valley
** Best-now $9-11

Uncomplicated; zesty fruit and spice tastes and scents

CHATEAU DE BAUN
1990 Russian River Valley Barrel Fermented
** Best-now $9-11

Lush and zesty; lots of fruit and honey

CHATEAU JULIEN
　　1990 Monterey County Barrel Fermented
　　** **Best-93-94 $9-11**
　　Robust, focused; some fruit and honey essences

CHATEAU SOUVERAIN
　　1990 Sonoma County Barrel Fermented
　　*** **Best-now $9-11**
　　Sturdy; lots of fruit and melon; delightful

CHATEAU SOUVERAIN
　　1991 Sonoma County Barrel Fermented
　　*** **Best-now $8-11**
　　Good on the palate; apple and pear scents

CHRISTOPHE
1990 California
** Best-now $6-8

Zesty and fruity; straight-forward

CONCHA Y TORO
1991 Maipo
** Best-now $5-7

Liberal fruit and flower scents and tastes; uncomplicated

CONGRESS SPRINGS
1990 Barrel-fermented Santa Clara County
** Best-now $8-10

Fruity, silky, and elegant with a flawless oak balance

COUSINO-MACUL
1991 Maipo
** Best-now $8-10

Lean fruit and spice scents and tastes; uncomplicated

COUSINO-MACUL
1990 Maipo Reserva
** Best-now $8-10
Generous butter and citrus flavors; rustic overtones; pleasant

CRESTON
1989 Paso Robles Barrel Fermented
** Best-now $9-11
Rich and flavorful; citrus and fruit tastes

DAVID WYNN
1992 Eden Valley
*** Best-now $9-11
Exotic fruit, honey, and spice aromas; mouthfilling; opulent

DOMAINE LA COLUMBETTE
1991 Vin du Paysone
*** Best-93-94 $9-11
Lots of fruit and floral scents; sound fruity flavor; full-bodied

DOMAINE MAS GUILHEM

1992   Vin du Pays d'Oc

***   Best-now $8-10

Aromas and flavors of citrus and flowers; brisk, medium body; good acidity

ERRAZURIZ

1991 Maule Valley Reserva

**   Best-now $8-10

Lots of toasty scents; modest oak and citrus tastes; tangy

ERRAZURIZ

1992   Maule Valley Reserva

***   Best-now   8-10

Flavorful fruit, spice, and vanilla; agreeable aromas; fresh and even

ESTANCIA

1990 Monterey

**   Best-now $7-10

Brisk, hearty, spicy, and toasty essences

ESTANCIA

1991 Monterey
***   Best-95-97 $7-9
*Pear scents and tastes; mellow spice;
silky texture*

FOPPIANO

1989 Sonoma County
**   Best-now $9-11
*Starts out a little heavy, but is supple
on the finish*

FREEMARK ABBEY

1989 Napa Valley
**   Best-now $9-11
*Elegant; tightly structured; lovely
balance of fruit and oak*

FRENCH CREEK

**1990 Columbia Valley Monterey
Vineyard**
**   Best-now $9-11
*Uncomplicated; more inorganic than
fruity*

GEYSER PEAK
1990 Sonoma County
** Best-now $7-9

Delicious, fresh fruity flavors

GLASS MOUNTAIN QUARRY
1989 Napa Valley
*** Best-now $7-9

Generous fruit and spice; focused; very tasty

HAWK CREST
1990 California
** Best-now $8-10

Uncomplicated, with fruity and zesty tastes

HAYWOOD
1990 California Vintner's Select
** Best-now $6-8

Brisk and tangy; fruit and vanilla overtones

HAYWOOD
1991 California Vintner's Select
**   Best-now $7-9

Smooth, light apple tastes; fresh and clean

HESS SELECT
1990 California
***   Best-now $8-11

Elegant with good depth and richness

HESS SELECT
1991 California
**   Best-now $9-11

Dry, modest citrus and fruit tastes; refreshing

HESS SELECTION
1991 California
***   Best-now $9-11

Appealing floral, appley scents; fruity, intense flavors

HOGUE
1991 Washington
***   **Best-now**   **$8-10**

Tropical flavors; very fresh and crisp; balanced

HOUGHTON
1991 Western Australia Wildflower Ridge
***   **Best-now**   **$8-9**

Tart citrus and fruit; delicate and harmonious

INGLENOOK
1990 Napa Valley
***   **Best-93-95**   **$9-11**

Sound, fresh fruit and citrus right to the finish

IVAN TAMAS
1990 Trebbiano Livermore
***   **Best-now**   **$8-10**

Rich fruit and honey; a touch of oak; luscious

J. FRITZ
1990 Dry Creek Valley
** Best-now $6-9
Tangy, fruity, and uncomplicated

JAMIESONS RUN
1992 Coonawarra
*** Best-now $9-11
Zesty, fruity, harmonious, and straight-forward

KENWOOD
1991 Sonoma Valley
*** Best-now $9-11
Clean, fruity, brisk, with good oak flavor

KONOCTI
1990 Lake Country
*** Best-now $9-11
Balanced, mouthfilling; zesty and fruity to the end

LAS VINAS
1990 California
***   **Best-now**   **$5-8**
*Appley chardonnay flavor; buttery
and toasty from barrel fermentation;
full-bodied*

LAWRENCE BARGETTO
1990 Central Coast Cypress
**   **Best-now**   **$6-9**
Fragrant, bold; mouthfilling

LOCKWOOD
1990 Monterey County
***   **Best-now**   **$7-9**
*Mouthfilling; harmonious blend of
fruit and citrus*

LOLONIS
1990 Mendocino County
**   **Best-now**   **$9-11**
*Mellow, flowery; lots of citrus; tangy,
brisk*

LOUIS MARTINI
1990 Napa Sonoma Counties
***   Best-now $8-10
Delicious; smooth tastes of fruit and spice

MADDALENA
1990 Central Coast
**   Best-now $6-9
Zesty and fruity with essence of oak

MADRONA
1989 El Dorado
**   Best-now $9-11
Hearty, rich with citrus and apple flavors

MCDOWELL VALLEY
1990 Mendocino
**   Best-now $8-10
Harmonious balance of fruit and citrus; zesty and lively

MCGILLIGAN BROTHERS
1992 Australian Bin 7000
** **Best-now** $7-9

Mature, flavorful; some citrus and spice taste

MEADOWGLEN
1990 California
** **Best-now** $8-10

Superior taste; smooth and buttery

MERIDIAN
1990 Santa Barbara
** **Best-now** $8-10

High quality fruit married to just the right amount of oak; great

MERIDIAN
1990 Santa Barbara County
*** **Best-now** $9-11

Fragrant, spicy aromas and flavors; lush and complex

MICHELTON ~~XXX~~ — Cost plus $5.99
    1992 Victoria
    *** Best-now $8-10
    Harmonious citrus, fruit, and herb
    aromas; agreeable honey and flowery
    tastes

MIGUEL TORRES
    1992 Curico District
    *** Best-now $8-9
    Fruit and citrus flavors; refreshing

MIRASSOU
    1991 Los Carneros
    *** Best-now 9-11
    Clean, zesty; good fruit at the end

MIRASSOU
    1990 Monterey County Fifth
    Generation Family Selection
    *** Best-now $9-11
    Harmonious pear and apple flavors
    with zesty overtones

MONTEREY VINEYARDS
1991 Classic
***　　**Best-now**　　**$5-7**
Brisk acidity; good fruit and floral tastes; flavorful

MOUNTAIN VIEW
1990 Monterey County
**　　**Best-now**　　**$5-7**
Harmonious, straight-forward; lots of fruit and spice

NAPA CELLARS
1990 Napa Valley
**　　**Best-now**　　**$6-8**
Zesty, oaky and uncomplicated

NAUTILUS
1991 Marlborough, New Zealand
***　　**Best-now**　　**$8-10**
Modest fruit; brisk essence of flowers; dry and brisk

NAVARRO
1989 Anderson Valley Table Wine
**   Best-now $6-9
Tart fruit aromas; zesty taste

NOMINEE
Paso Robles Central Coast 1992
***   Best-now $5-7
Zesty, fruity, and uncomplicated

NOZZOLE
1991 Vigneto le Bruniche
***   Best-94-95 $9-11
Good fruit and spice; clean, refreshing

OAK FALLS
1991 Napa Valley Private Reserve
**   Best-now $6-8
Citrus and fruit in a sound blend

OXFORD LANDING
1992   South Eastern Australia
***   Best-now $7-9
Voluptuous with exotic fruit aromas;
fruity, clean flavors

PAUL THOMAS
1991 Columbia Valley
***   Best-now $9-11
Flavorful, brisk, fruit and citrus
scents and tastes

PEDRONCELLI
1990 Reserve Dry Creek Valley
***   Best-now $8-10
Agreeable fruit aroma and flavor;
brisk

PHILLIPE-LORRAINE
1990 Napa Valley
**   Best-now $9-11
Dry, tasty, zesty with nice citrus
tastes

PRINCE MICHEL
1991 Virginia
***   Best-now $9-11

Fresh, clean, citrus tastes; harmonious

PURPLE MOUNTAIN
1991 Monterey Barrel Fermented
**   Best-now $9-11

Mature, direct, and a little inorganic

Q.C. FLY
1991 California
**   Best-now $8-10

Oaky and fruity with a bit of complexity

RIVERSIDE FARM
1990 California
**   Best-now $6-8

Harmonious and clean; mouthfilling

RODNEY STRONG
   1990 Sonoma County
   ** **Best-now** $8-10
   More spice than most, but clean and refreshing

RODNEY STRONG
   1991 Sonoma County
   *** **Best-now** $8-9
   Uncomplicated; mellow blend of fruit and vanilla

ROO'S LEAP
   1991 Coonawarra Barrel Fermented
   ** **Best-now** $9-11
   Tasty; some fruit and citrus scents

ROSEMOUNT
   1991 Hunter Valley Australia
   *** **Best-now** $9-11
   Gutsey, appley, toasty accents; very tasty

ROSEMOUNT
1991 Hunter Valley Australia Diamond Label
***   Best-now $9-11
Sturdy, apple and toasty oak accents; mouthfilling

ROSEMOUNT
1991 Hunter Valley Matured in Oak Casks
**   Best-now   8-10
Tasty; good oak tastes; not much fruit; earthy at the end

ROSEMOUNT
1991 Southeastern Australia Matured in Oak
***   Best-now $8-11
Harmonious blend of spice and fruit

ROUND HILL
1991 California
**   Best-now $5-7
Zestful, fresh, harmonious, citrusy tastes

RUSTRIDGE
1990 Napa Valley
**   Best-93-95 $9-11
The pineapple jumps out; brisk fruit and spice scents and tastes

RUTHERFORD ESTATE
1990 Napa Valley
**   Best-now $7-9
Refreshing with smooth zesty and fruity tastes

RUTHERFORD ESTATE CELLARS
1990 Napa Valley
***   Best-now $5-7
Apple tartness; oaky and toasty; crisp

RYECROFT
1992   Flame Tree McLaren Vale
***   Best-now $8-10
Robust, graceful, delicious

SEBASTIANI
1988 Sonoma County
***   Best-now $7-9
Concentrated berry flavors; fruity, balanced

SEGHESIO
1990Sonoma and
Mendocino Counties
**   Best-now $8-10
A citrusy, uncomplicated, straight-forward Chardonnay

SEPPELT
1991 Southeastern Australia
Reserve Bin
**   Best-now $7-9
Luscious, delicate, sturdy fruit and pineapple tastes along with nice oak

SILVERADO HILL CELLARS
1990 Napa Valley
***   Best-93-94 $9-11
Harmonious, tart; lots of fragrance

SODA CANYON
1990 Napa County 12th Leaf
***   Best-94-95 $9-11

Firm and balanced; zesty; honey and fruit flavors

SONOMA CREEK
1989 Carneros Barrel Fermented
****   Best-now $9-11

Mouthfilling with complex fruit and citrus tastes

ST ANDREWS WINERY
1990 Napa Valley
**   Best-now $9-11

Uncomplicated; balanced fruit and spice essences

ST FRANCIS
1990 Sonoma County
***   Best-93-94 $9-11

Supple, rich; lots of oak and fruit; tasty

STEPHEN ZELLERBACH
1990 Sonoma County
***   Best-now $8-10

Luscious blend of zesty fruit and vanilla tastes

STEVENOT
1990 California
**   Best-now $6-9

Delicate smoothness with fruit flavors; uncomplicated

STONE CREEK
1988 Estate Bottled Alexander Valley
**   Best-now $8-10

Well-balanced, elegant, cream and vanillin

STONELEIGH
1991 Marlborough
***   Best-now $9-11

Fruit; some oak and buttery aromas; flavorful fruit tastes

SUTTER HOME
1990 California
*** Best-now $5-7
*Clean and uncomplicated; fruity
essences; zesty*

TAFT STREET
1990 Sonoma County
** Best-now $9-11
*Uncomplicated blend of fruit and
spice aromas*

TAGARIS
1990 Columbia Valley Barrel
Fermented
** Best-93-95 $8-9
Fresh, focused fruit, spice, and herbs

TYRREL'S
1991 Chardonnay-Semillon South
Eastern Australia Long Flat
** Best-now $6-9
*Supple fig, mint, honey, and herbs;
refreshing*

VICHON
1991 California Coastal Selection
**   **Best-now** $9-11

Fruity and spicy scents and tastes; silky texture

VILLA MT EDEN
1990 California Cellar Select
**   **Best-now** $7-9

Mellow, zesty fruit tastes

VILLA MT EDEN
1991 California Cellar Select
***   **Best-now** $9-11

Mature, direct, and fruity; harmonious

WHITEHALL LANE
1990 Napa Valley Le Petit
**   **Best-now** $7-9

Mouthfilling fruit and honey; zesty finish

WILDHURST
1990 Napa
***   **Best-now**   **$9-11**
Mature fruit aromas and flavors;
flavorful

WILDHURST
1990 Napa Valley
***   **Best-now**   **$9-11**
Luscious and uncomplicated; mature
fruit and oak

ZACA MESA
1990 Santa Barbara County
***   **Best-now**   **$9-11**
Delicious, flavorful, fruity, and
citrusy

Chenin Blanc

ESTATE BOTTLED

Beringer.

CHENIN BLANC

NAPA VALLEY

GROWN, PRODUCED AND
BOTTLED BY BERINGER
VINEYARDS B.W. 46

ST. HELENA, CALIFORNIA
ALCOHOL 11.9% BY VOL.
750 ML

The grape of the Loire Valley of France, the grape of Vouvray. It is also blended into other wines. In the United States, it is vinified by itself to make wines that range from dry to slightly sweet. It is a fresh, lively wine that occasionally has a slight fizz. Serve the dry ones with light fish or seafood; the sweeter ones could be served with ham, chicken salads, and cold soups.

BERINGER   *BEST BUY*
1991 Proprietor's Grown
***   **Best-now**   **$5-7**
Lively, clean; off-dry; loaded with
flower and fruit scents

DANIEL GEHRS   *BEST BUY*
1991 Le Cheniere Monterey
****   **Best-93-95**   **$7-9**
Elegant; dry; lots of fruit and honey;
aromatic flower scents

DE MARTINO
1990 Maipo Valley Santa Inez Vineyard
***   **Best-94-96**   **$4-6**
Sturdy, focused fruit and spice tastes;
firm texture; a touch of chocolate at
the finish

HUSCH VINEYARDS
1991 Mendocino
***　　Best-now　　$8-10

*Medium dry; fruit and flower scents
and tastes; delicate*

PRESTON VINEYARDS
1991 Dry Creek
***　　Best-now　　$6-8

*Nicely dry; lush fruit for a delightful
treat*

SIMI
1991 Mendocino
***　　Best-now　　$6-8

*Aromatic nose; brisk and flowery;
soft*

STAG'S LEAP WINERY
1991 Napa Valley
****　　Best-now　　$5-7

Focused grapy flavors; balanced

Chianti

BORGHI D'ELSA

1991

CHIANTI

DENOMINAZIONE DI ORIGINE CONTROLLATA E GARANTITA

DRY RED WINE

BOTTLED BY MELINI s.c.a.r.l. CALMASINO
AT ITS OWN CELLARS OF GAGGIANO - ITALIA

PRODUCT OF ITALY

𝔐elini®

Net Cont. 750 ml   Alc. 12% by vol.

A region of Tuscany, the Chianti area has been reclassified to the highest quality category of wine origin. This has done wonders for the quality of the wine which is being produced. There are fewer straw basket bottles, but more good Chianti in conventional bottles. The Sangoviese is the principal grape used, and the addition of other grapes is strictly limited. Riservas have been aged in wood at least three years and tend to be more expensive. Regular Chianti can be very good, light, and medium-bodied. Serve with pizza (of course), pastas, spicy sausage, game birds, and steak.

MELINI   *BEST BUY*
   1990 Borghi d'Elsa Chianti
   **   **Best-now**   **$4-6**
   Round; even complex flavors

CASTELLO BANFI
   1988 Classico Riserva
   **   **Best-now**   **$9-11**
   Rich, zesty; some cherry notes

FATTORIA MONTELLORI
1990 Chianti
**Best-93-95 $6-8

*Sound; tannic; lots of berry and
cherry to savor*

PIDERI DI GRETOLE
1989 Classico
**   Best-now $8-10

*Uncomplicated; good berry scents
and tastes*

RUFFINO
1989 Aziano Vineyard Chianti Classico
****   Best-now $9-11

*Spice and raspberry aromas and
flavors; soft "old" style*

Gewürztraminer

Grown now in Washington State and California, the Gewürztraminer grape is the main varietal grown in Alsace. The Alsatian wines tend to be very dry with lots of floral and spice aroma and flavors. The United States tends to produce less dry, sweeter wines that still retain the spice that is a hallmark of this variety. Brisk and lively, they do well with oriental foods, and other spicy dishes

BERINGER   *BEST BUY*
1991 North Coast Gewürztraminer
*** **Best-now** **$4-7**
Minty, spicy flavors and aromas;
slightly sweet, refreshing acid
balance

CLOS DU BOIS *BEST BUY*
1990 Early Harvest
Gewürztraminer Alexander Valley
**** **Best-now** **$7-9**
A rich wine characterized by distinct
apricot aroma and flavor; balanced
acidity; spicey and candied fruit
finish

ADLER FELS
1991 Sonoma County
** **Best-now** **$8-9**
Uncomplicated, rich; good spice and
fruit

ALEXANDER VALLEY
VINEYARDS
1992 Gewürztraminer
Alexander Valley
** **Best-now** **$7-9**
Spicy scents and tastes with good
fruitiness; fresh

CLAIBORNE & CHURCHILL
1991 Central Coast Dry Alsatian Style
**   Best-now $8-10

Tart, concentrated, flowers and citrus accents

DAVIS BYNUM
1990 Russian River Gewürztraminer
***** Best-now $7-10

Rose petals, intense sachet aroma and flavors; complex and long on the finish

DE LOACH
1991 Russian River Valley Early Harvest
**   Best-now $8-10

Brisk fruit and citrus; only slightly sweet

FIRESTONE
1991 California
**** Best-now $7-9

Zesty, flowery; lots of fruit and citrus; concentrated and robust

HUSCH
1991 Gerwurztraminer
Anderson Valley
*   **Best-now** $7-9
Brisk, concentrated; lots of citrus and spice

ST FRANCIS
1991 Gerwurztraminer
Sonoma County
**   **Best-now** $9-11
Clean, appley, fruity and flavorful

THOMAS FOGARTY
1991 Monterey Ventana Vineyards
**   **Best-now** $9-11
Zesty, citrusy; on the dry side

Merlot

ALEXANDER
VALLEY

MERLOT

ESTATE BOTTLED

1990

ALEXANDER VALLEY
VINEYARDS

By itself, Merlot produces wine with dark, rich red color with plum and raspberry tastes. Generally low in tannin, it can be stout and tight. The United States, Chile and Australia produce good inexpensive Merlots. In France, it is used for blending. Most should be ready to drink now. Goes well with lamb, grilled fish, steak, and duck.

BEL ARBORS *BEST BUY*
   1990 California
   *** **Best-94-95** **$6-8**
   Delicate; fragrant with berry and
   cherry overtones; heavy on tannins

DOMAINE
DE L'ARJOLLE *BEST BUY*
   1991 Vin du Pays Cotes de
   Thongues
   *** **Best-93-96** **$7-9**
   Good aroma of herbs and berries;
   almost chewy; luscious

DOMAINE LA NOBLE *BEST BUY*
   1990 Pays de l'Aude
   **** **Best-now** **$5-6**
   Intense black currant; ripe plum
   flavors; complex, excellent balance

JACOB'S CREEK *BEST BUY*
   1990 South Eastern Autralia
   **** **Best-now** **$6-7**
   Intense, complex fruit flavors; rich,
   well-balanced

ROUND HILL *BEST BUY*
   1990 California
   ***   Best-now $6-8
   *Nice harmonious blend of cherry
   scents and flavors*

**RUTHERFORD
RANCH** *BEST BUY*
   1990 Napa Valley
   ***   Best-94-95 $7-9
   *Zesty cherry and oak essence; clean,
   taut, refreshing*

SEBASTIANI *BEST BUY*
   1990 Sonoma County
   ****   Best-now $8-10
   *Intense ripe black currant and pepper
   flavors; fairly high alcohol; soft
   tannins*

BONVERRE
NV California Famille Lot No.
*** **Best-now** **$7-9**
Lively; modest tannins; good fruit and spice; very agreeable

CARA VIEJA
1991 Maule Valley
** **Best-now** **$4-6**
Agreeable fruit and berry scents and tastes; delicate and clean

CHATEAU JULIEN
1991 Monterey County
*** **Best-94-96** **$9-11**
Mature fruit; hard tannins and herbal essence

CHATEAU SOUVERAIN
1991 Alexander Valley
*** **Best-94-96** **$9-11**
Mellow, generous; good fruit; some herb tastes

CONCHA Y TORO
1989 Rapel Marques de Casa Concha Peumo Vineyard
** Best-93-95 $9-11

Liberal berry and currant scents and tastes; concentrated and sound

COVEY RUN
1989 Yakima Valley
*** Best-now $7-9

Intense, focused, spicy, and berry flavors; some complexity

DOMAINE CAPION
1991 Vin de Pays d'Oc
*** Best-93-97 $6-8

Mature fruit aromas and flavors; full-bodied; silky, and aggreeable

DOMAINE LE NOBLE
1991 Pays de l'Aude
*** Best-now $5-7

Raspberry, fruity scents and flavors; clean, intense

ERRAZURIZ
1990 Maule Valley
**   Best-93-95 $7-9

Solid berry and currant scents and tastes; good tannins; lively

ERRAZURIZ
1991 Maule Valley
**   Best-94-95 $7-8

Flavorful, currant, berry tastes; good tannins

ERRAZURIZ
1992   Maule Valley
***   Best-now $7-9

Focused berry and herb scents and tastes; firm fruit; straight forward

J. LOHR
1991 California Cypress
**   Best-now $8-10

Lush cherry; refreshing, light, and uncomplicated

MIRASSOU
1990 Monterey County Fifth Generation Family Selection
**   Best-now $8-11

Simple; low tannin; fruit and herb tastes

MONTEREY VINEYARDS
1990 Classic
***   Best-93-95 $5-7

Replete with mellow chocolate and berry scents and tastes; solid

MOONDANCE
1990 Napa Valley
***   Best-93-96 $9-11

Lithe and focused; currant and cherry scents and tastes

OAK FALLS
1990 Napa Valley Private Reserve
**   Best-93-95 $7-9

Harmonious combining of tabacco and fruitiness; silky with a little tannin

PARDUCCI
1990 North Coast
**   Best-now $7-9

Heavy tannins but solid; some cedary taste

RAPIDAL RIVER
1991 Virginia
*   Best-now $8-10

Full-bodied blend of spice, oak, and a little chocolate; good tannins

RAVENSWOOD
1991 North Coast Vintner's Blend
**   Best-94-96 $8-11

Appealing and lively berry and fruit, but wait on the tannins

SAN PEDRO LONTUE
1989 Chile
**   Best-now $6-8

Blackberry scents, light body; fruity; slightly tart

SANTA CAROLINA
1989 Chile
**   Best-now $4-6

*Medium-full body; good depth of
fruit; ripe berry flavors; light oak and
light tannins*

SANTA RITA
1989 Maipo Valley "120" Label
***   Best-now $4-6

*Big, fruity, spicy merlot scents; soft
tannins*

SARTORI
1989 Grave del Fruili
**   Best-now $5-6

Delicate, tobacco and cedar to savor

SEBASTIANI
1991 Sonoma County
***   Best-now $7-9

*Clean, zesty, fruit and berry scents
and tastes*

SERGIO TRAVERSO
1990 Colchagua
**   **Best-now**   **$5-7**
Lots of fruit; pepper and tobacco harmoniously blended

STEVENOT
1989 North Coast Reserve
**   **Best-now**   **$5-7**
Big, black currant flavors; herbal, balanced

TRENTADUE
1987 Sonoma
***   **Best-94-01**   **$7-9**
Focused and full-bodied; generous fruit; bold and flavorful

WILDHURST
1991 Clear Lake
***   **Best-94-95**   **$7-9**
Flavorful; sound blend of berry and tannin scents and tastes

Petite Sirah

One of the oldest varieties in California, it was thought to be the famous Syrah grape of the Rhone Valley. It was named Petite Sirah in the United States In fact, the grape turned out to be the Duriff, a blending grape in the Rhone. It has been used as a blender in California, but now vintners are making sturdy, rich, dark wine, replete with berry and pepper flavors. Try with steak, game, and aged and goat cheeses.

TRENTADUE   *BEST BUY*
   1991 Sonoma
   ****   Best-93-10 $9-11
   Mature berry, pepper, and spice
   scents; focused fruit; good tannins;
   should age well

FOPPIANO
   1990 Petite Sirah Sonoma County
   ***   Best-93-96 $9-11
   Focused and luscious; hints of berries
   and spice

MARRIETTA
   1988 Petite Sirah Sonoma County
   **   Best-now $8-10
   A full-bodied, spicy, zesty wine with
   loads of fruit

MIRASSOU
1989 Petite Sirah Fifth Generation Selection Monterey
***　　Best-now　　$6-8

Berry aromas; soft tannins; jammy blueberry and cherry fruit tastes

PARDUCCI
1988 Petite Sirah Mendocino
**　　Best-now　　$5-7

An amazing little wine; packed with fruit and spice

RABBIT RIDGE
1990 Petite Sirah Sonoma County
**　　Best-now　　$9-11

Chocolate on the finish; full-bodied plum and grape scents

TRENTADUE
1987 Alexander Valley
****　Best-98-05　$9-11

Exhuberant berry, spice and pepper scents; moderate tannins; full-bodied; lay this away

Pinot Noir/Bordeaux

1991

Parducci

PINOT NOIR

MENDOCINO COUNTY

Pinot Noir is the grape of the great wines of Burgundy. In Burgundy, there is no blending of varieties, only the Pinot Noir, a grape with tender skin, subject to all sorts of mildew, fungus, and assorted diseases. In addition, it likes a very even climate; too much hot weather and it will lose its great nose and complex tastes. California, Washington, and Oregon are producing wine of medium body with focused flavors and tannins. They are moving ever upward in quality as the winemakers learn more about this difficult grape. In Burgundy, the centuries have brought dividends to the grapes along the Cote d'Or, where some of the greatest wines in the world are produced. These are rich, dark red, graceful with sturdy tannins; almost chewy. Serve with grilled meats and fish, duck, and the milder cheeses.

BICHOT
1989 Pinot Noir Bourgogne Chateau de Dracey
**   **Best-now**   **$8-10**
Ripe fruit tastes; silky, uncomplicated, and tasty

BICHOT
1989 Pinot Noir Bourgogne Chateau de Montpatey
***   **Best-now**   **$9-11**
Focused fruit and berry tastes; pleasant spice and pepper overtones

BRIDGEVIEW
1991 Pinot Noir Williamette Valley
**   Best-now $5-7
Good berry and vanilla scents and tastes; soft and smooth

CHATEAU BELAIR
1987 Haut-Medoc
**   Best-now $6-8
Deliciously soft; fruity and elegant

DROUHIN "LA FORET"
1990 Burgundy Pinot Noir
***   Best-now $8-11
Strong black currant scents; very burgundian

LABOURE-ROI
1990 Bourgogne Rouge
**   Best-now $9-11
Light and extremely fruity; more like Beaujolais than burgundy; fresh, well-made

Red

These are wines that do not easily fit into the established categories in this book. Vintners of all countries are experimenting with various blends, producing very good wines that have names like Meritage, Pinotage, and others. The wines so classified are listed here because they meet the "taste tests" applied to all others in this book. They deserve consideration as serious as the other classifications. In general, they will go well with red meats, medium and strong cheeses, and grilled fowl.

BODEGAS PEDRO ROVIRA   *BEST BUY*
1987 Tarragona Catalonia Reserve
** **Best-now** $5-7
Ripe, earthy, herbal and zesty

CHATEAU DE CALAGE   *BEST BUY*
1991 Coteaux du Languedoc
**** **Best-93-97** $7-9
Concentrated berry and licorice aromas; bold, with low tannins; voluptuous

DOMAINE CAPION   *BEST BUY*
1991 Vin de Pays d'Oc
*** **Best-93-97** $6-8
Gentle tastes of spice and concentrated fruit; smooth texture

DOMAINE DE CLAIRFONT   *BEST BUY*
1991 Vin de Pays de Vaucluse
** **Best-now** $5-6
Plum and pepper tastes; clean and intense

GEORGES DUBOEUF   *BEST BUY*
1992 Chiroubles Chateau de Javernand
****   Best-now $5-7
Sturdy and rich; lots of fruit; silky finish

KLINE CONTRA   *BEST BUY*
1990 Costa Carigne
****   Best-93-96 $8-11
Dense; intense black currants; balanced; ready now; years to go.

TRENTADUE   *BEST BUY*
1991 "Old Patch Red" Alexander Valley
****   Best-now $9-11
Full-bodied; fruit, pepper, and spice aromas and flavors; bold and clean

TRENTADUE   *BEST BUY*
1992   Salute and Augury
****   Best-93-98 $6-8
Elegant, silky fruit, cherry, and tannins; mouthfilling

ABADIA DEL BROBLE
1990 La Macha Fermin Ayuso
** Best-now $5-7

*Tart, fresh; some herbs and spice;
very light color*

ARCIERO
1989 Santa Barbara Nebbiolo
*** Best-now $9-11

*Complex leathery, oaky, nutty
flavors; nicely balanced; rich fruit
flavors*

BANDIERA
1988 Napa Valley
*** Best-now $5-7

*Cedar, bell pepper, cherry and tar;
pleasant texture; medium body;
flavors of cherries, cassis and
peppers; spicy finish*

BARBARESCO RESERVE
1985 Ovello Vineyard
***   Best-now $7-9

Cedar, anise, earthy scents; rich, intense berry flavors

BERSIG
1990 Pinotage South Africa Breede River Valley
***   Best-now $8-9

Sturdy and brisk; flowery aromas

BODEGAS CASTANO
1987 Pozuelo Crianza Cosecha Yecla
**   Best-now $7-9

Zesty, intense, tobacco and cherry scents and tastes

BODEGAS CUEVA DEL GRANERO
1988 La Mancha Crianza
**   Best-now $5-7

Simple blend of berries and peppers; very palatable

BODEGAS FAUSTINO MARTINEZ
1989 Rioja
** Best-now $9-11
Sturdy, zesty; plenty of fruit and spice

BODEGAS LOS LLANOS
1987 Valdepenas Crianza en Roble
Senorio de los Llanos Reserva
** Best-now $8-10
Spicy, fragrant; taste of cherries

BODEGAS MAESE JOAN
1986 Rioja Armorial Crianza
** Best-now $7-8
Mellow spice and herbs, but not much fruit

BODEGAS MARTINEZ BUJANDA
1988 Rioja Conde de Valdemar
Crianza
*** Best-93-96 $7-10
Zesty scents and tastes of berries and fruit

BODEGAS MARTINEZ BUJANDA
1991 Rioja Valdemar Vino Tinto
** Best-now $6-8
Flowery, refreshing; scents and tastes of berries and fruit

BODEGAS PEDORO ROVIRA
1982 Tarragona Vino Tinto Gran Reserva
** Best-now $9-11
Soft, ripe essences of berries, tobacco and toast; elegant

BONNY DOON
1990 Ca del Solo California Big House Red
*** Best-now $6-9
Tangy and fruity, but mainly tangy; delicious

BONNY DOON
1992 Clos de Gilroy California Grenache
***   Best-93-94 $7-9
Luscious berry and fruit; graceful, medium-bodied

BONNY DOON
1992 Grenache California Clos de Gilroy
***   Best-now $7-9
Lots of pepper, very little fruit; clean, brisk

BONNY DOON
1992 Vin Gris De Cigare
***   Best-now $5-7
Good berry and fruit, flower scented and dry

BOSCAINI SOAVE CLASSICO
1989 Montelone Vineyard
***   Best-now $8-10
Fruity plum flavor; clean, fresh, balanced

BOUCHARD PERE ET FILS
1983 Chambolle Musigny
**   Best-now $8-10

Nice, round, mature Pinot Noir flavors; amazing complexity given the price and vintage; soft, elegant, at its peak

CAMPO VIEJO
1985 Reserva Rioja Spain
**   Best-now $8-10

A classic Rioja red with elegant Tempranillo fruit, followed by layers of oak and light tannins

CANTINA ZACCAGNINI
1988 Montepulciano d'Abruzzo
**   Best-now $8-10

A beefy and rich velvety wine filled with berry, fruit, and lots of mild, "purple teeth" tannins; gorgeous

CAVES VELHAS
1978 Garrafeira Portugal
** Best-93-95 $9-11

The round, soft fatness of the Periquita grape marries wonderfully with the intense, tannic structure of the Tinta Miuda grape

CHATEAU BOUSQUETTE
1989 St. Chinian
** Best-now $9-11

Hearty, scented; some berry and fruitiness

CHATEAU DE BOHOMME
1991 Minervois
*** Best-93-95 $6-8

Mellow cherry aroma and taste; a simple but mouthfilling wine

CHATEAU DE CASENOVE
1990 Cote du Roussillon
**** Best-93-95 $9-11

Exhuberant; toasty cherry and cedar aromas; harmonious fruit; medium body

CHATEAU DE FONTANCHE
1990 St. Chinian Cuvee Grand Veneur
** Best-now $6-8

Heavily scented, even, zesty, piquant

CHATEAU DE LUC
1990 Corbieres
*** Best-94-95 $4-6

Brisk and distinct; zesty and fruity scents and taste

CHATEAU LA BORONNE
1990 Corbieres
*** Best-93-96 $7-9

Flowers, spice, and cherry scents; chewy, mature fruit tastes; exhuberant

CLINE
1990 Carignane Contra Costa County
*** **Best-now** **$8-9**
Fruit, spice, and berry in liberal quantities; silky

CLINE
1990 Cotes d'Oakley Contra Costa County
*** **Best-now** **$6-9**
Harmonious blend of berries, herbs and tannins

CLOS FERDINAND
1990 Vin du Pays de Thongue
*** **Best-93-95** **$6-8**
Focused berry and toasty scents; downy texture; delicious

CLOS LA CONTALE
1990 Cahors
*** **Best-93-97** **$9-11**
Aromas of cherry and leather; mellow, intense fruit flavors and nice tannins; silky texture

COMMANDERIE DE LA BARGEMONE
1990 Coteaux d'Aix en Provence
*** Best-now $6-8
Mature cherry scents; soft texture; lush fruit

COMMANDERIE DE LA BARGEMONE
1990 Rose Provence
** Best-now $7-9
Very flavorful for a rose; goes well with a wide range of foods

CONCHA Y TORO
1989 Marques de Casa Concho, Peumo Vineyard, Rapel, Chile
*** Best-now $7-9
Licorice, flowers, spice; nice balance of plummy fruit, acid, and oak; medium body, luscious finish

CONTI SERRISTORI
1990 Orvieto Classico Secco
** Best-now $4-6
Clean, crisp, nicely balanced flavors; lively

CORBIERES
1991 Les Producteurs Du Mont Tauch
** Best-now $6-9
Sound cherry tastes; earthy on the finish

COUCHEROY
1989 Graves
*** Best-93-95 $8-10
Excellent tobacco and cassis flavors; saturated and delicate flavor

DAVID BRUCE
1990 Mrs. Baggins California
*** Best-now $9-11
Harmonious; tannic; some taste of fruit also

DOMAINE BOIS MONSIEUR
NV Coteaux do Langedoc
***   Best-now $6-8

Mature currant and spice tastes; pleasant and smooth

DOMAINE CLAVEL
1991 Le Mejanelle Coteaux de Languedoc
***   Best-93-95 $7-9

Firm, uncomplicated and pleasant; intense fruit

DOMAINE D'AUPILHAC
1991 Vin du Pays Mont Baudile
****   Best-94-96 $8-10

Mature scents of cassis; mellow fruitiness; sound and tasty

DOMAINE DE CAZAL-VIEL
1990 St. Chinian
***   Best-now $6-8

Ripe cherry and spice scents and tastes; pleasant and tasty

DOMAINE DE CAZAL-VIEL
1991 St. Chinian
***   Best-now $6-8
Zesty cherry flavors; medium body;
silky and even on the finish

DOMAINE DE CAZAL-VIEL
1991 St. Chinian Cuvee
Georges A. Aouest
***   Best-93-98 $9-11
Mature fruit and pepper scents and
tastes; exhuberant and lush

DOMAINE DE CHAMPAGNA
1991 Cotes du Ventoux
***   Best-now $6-8
Aromatic, silky; mature fruit and
medium body

DOMAINE DE L'AMEILLAUD
1990 Vaucluse
**   Best-93-95 $4-6
Very aromatic; good berry fruit with
that hint of anise that suggests a
Chateauneuf du Pape

DOMAINE DE L'ANTENET
   1990 Cahors
   ***   Best-93-97 $9-11
   Aromatic cassis; spice and herbal
   aromas; mature fruit and spice tastes

DOMAINE DE POUY
   1990 Ugni Blanc Cotes de Gascogne
   **   Best-now $5-6
   Fruity and dry; very classy

DOMAINE DES ANGES
   1990 Cotes du Ventoux
   ***   Best-93-96 $8-10
   Smooth, dark fruit and smoke
   aromas; savory finish

DOMAINE PERRIERE
   1990 Vin de Pays de l'Aude Les
   Amandiers
   **   Best-now $4-6
   Brisk finish preceded by berry and
   oak scents and tastes; uncomplicated

DOMAINE ST GEORGES
1988 Corbieres Grand Millesime Elevee en Futs de Chene
**   Best-now $7-9

Silky; harmonious blend of spice and plum

DUXOUP WINEWORKS
1991 Napa Gamay Dry Creek Valley
***   Best-now $8-10

Full-bodied, harmonious; zesty, fruity, with good tannins

EGRI BIKAVER
1987 Hungary
**   Best-now $5-7

Light, grapey, balanced; tomato scent and flavors

FARINA
1990 Toro Tinto
**   Best-now $7-9

Clean, luscious; some plum tastes

FETZER
NV California Premium Red
*** **Best-now** **$7-9**
*Fragrant berry nose; balanced, fresh,
soft; 1.5 Liter jug*

FETZER
1990 Red Table Wine Mendocino County Organically Grown Grapes
** **Best-now** **$8-10**
*Uncomplicated; sound fruit and berry
scents and tastes; good oak notes*

GEORGES DUBOEUF
1992 Chenas Flower Label
*** **Best-now** **$7-9**
*Opulent berry aromas; mature fruit;
exhuberant finish*

GEORGES DUBOEUF
1992 Chiroubles Flower Label
*** **Best-now** **$7-9**
*Aromatic fruit, mineral, and floral
scents; brisk and elegant; smooth*

GRAN CORPAS
1988 Tarragone
***   **Best-now** $5-7
Zesty, focused, silky, and full-bodied; herb and cherry tastes

HALLCREST
1990 Clos de Jeanine California
***   **Best-now** $6-8
Focused berry and cherry scents and tastes; even and a little tart

HARDY'S
1990 Shiraz Cabernet South Eastern Australia Captain's Selection
**   **Best-93-94** $5-7
Luscious, hearty, and fruity

HIJOS DE ANTONIO BARCELO
1991 Riberade Duero Vina Major Tinto
***   **Best-now** $6-8
Luscious, zesty berry flavors

JAUME SERRA
1989 Penedes Crianza
** Best-now $6-9

Supple blend of berry and fruit scents and tastes

JOSE MARIA DE FONSECA
1987 Periquita Portugal
** Best-now $6-8

Very full and round; ripe red fruits; similar to a heavy handed Chateauneuf du Pape

KLEINDALL
1990 Pinotage Stellenbosch
** Best-now $8-9

Cherry, cedar, and fruit scents and tastes

MAISON L'AIGLON
1990 St-Chinian Grand Reserve
** Best-93-94 $5-7

Lively, flavorful, currant taste; harmonious

MARQUES DE CACERES
1989 Rioja
*** **Best-now** **$8-10**
Lots of berry scents and tastes; sound and balanced

MICHELTON
1991 Cabernet/Shiraz/Merlot Victoria
*** **Best-93-96** **$8-10**
Mellow berry and smoke aromas; moderate body; flavorful

MITCHELTON
1992 Cab Mac MCM Mitchelton Victoria
** **Best-now** **$8-10**
Lots of berry accents; clean and even

MONT TUCH
1989 Fitou
*** **Best-now** **$6-9**
Spicy, fruity, soft, big flavors; uncomplicated

MONTEREY VINEYARDS
1990 Classic
*** **Best-now** $4-6
*Mouthfilling; delicate texture; good
berry, pepper, and spice*

MONTROSE
1991 Poet's Corner South Eastern
Australia
** **Best-95-97 $5-7**
*Dark cherry background to a
fragrant uncomplicated dry wine*

NAVARRO CORREAS
1988 Malbec Mendoza
** **Best-now $9-11**
*Even fruitiness; ripe flavors; deli-
cious*

PELLIGRINI FAMILY
1991 Cotes de Sonoma Sonoma
County Deux Cepages
** **Best-now $5-7**
*Replete with berries, spices, and fruit;
delightful*

PERQUITA
1989 Azeitao
**   Best-now $4-6
Uncomplicated silky smoothness;
slight Port overtones

PIO CESARE
1989 Rosso del Piemonte
***   Best-now $8-10
Intense, complex, herbal dried fruit
flavors; soft, balanced

POLIZIANO
1990 Rosso de Montepulciano
**   Best-now $9-11
Pepper and spices are preceded by
sturdy berry and currant scents and
tastes

PRESTON VINEYARDS
1991 Faux Castel Rouge
***   Best-93-95 $9-11
Gentle finish, supple; spice and
peppers to savor

PRESTON VINEYARDS
1990 Faux-Castel Rouge Dry Creek Valley
**   Best-94-95 $8-11
Earthy, strong tannins; good berry tastes

R.H. PHILLIPS
1990 Alliance California
**   Best-now $9-11
Sturdy structure; mature fruit, cherry, and oak; balanced, tasty

RABBIT RIDGE
1989 Allure California
**   Best-now $6-8
Mellow spice and cherry tastes; uncomplicated; earthy finish

RABBIT RIDGE
1989 Allure Proprietary Red Wine
***   Best-now $8-10
Soft texture; balanced berry and pepper aromas and tastes; flavorful

RENE BARBIER
NV Penedes Mediterranean Red
**   Best-now $4-6

Mellow, delicate, cherry and vanilla scents and tastes

RESERVE DU PRESIDENT
1989 Vin De Corse Corsica
**   Best-now $6-8

A mouthful of ripe fruit and sweet spicy flavors

SALVADOR POREDA
1987 Vina Vermeta Tinto Reserva Monastrell Alicante
**   Best-now $8-10

Scents and tastes of berries and tobacco; brisk

SANTA CAROLINA
1989 Merlot and Maipo Valley Santa Rosa Vineyard
**   Best-95-97 $5-7

Luscious, mature fruity tastes

SANTA CRISTINA
1989 Tuscan Red Table Wine
***   Best-now $8-10
Scents of roses; black cherry flavors;
fresh acidity and softness

SEBASTIANI
1989 Cabernet Franc Sonoma
County
***   Best-93-95 $9-11
Full-bodied; delicate blend of fruit
and currant tastes

ST. MARTIN
1989 Reserve Mourvedre
**   Best-now $5-7
Fresh, ripe; blueberry fruit; vibrant
purple color; bistro style

TOPOLOS
1989 Alicante Bouschet Russian
River Valley
***   Best-now $9-11
Organically produced; mature, firm
texture; focused

TOPOLOS
1990 Alicante Bouschet Russian River Valley
***   Best-now $9-11
Organically produced; mature, firm texture; focused

TOPOLOS
1988 Grand Noir Sonoma
***   Best-93-96 $7-9
Focused fruit and earthy scents and tastes; flavorful

TRAPICHE
1988 Malbec Mendoza Oak Cask Reserve
**   Best-now $7-9
Fresh, fruity and full-bodied

TRENTADUE
1988 "Old Patch Red" Alexander Valley
**   Best-now $7-9
Strong, hearty, and robust

TRENTADUE
1988 Carignane Alexander Valley
***   Best-93-99 $7-9
Sturdy; lots of fruit, spice and pepper;
rich, mouthfilling

TRENTADUE
1991 Carignane Alexander Valley
***   Best-94-98 $9-11
Firm spice and cherry scents;
graceful, tasty

TRENTADUE
NV Red Table Wine California
***   Best-93-96 $5-7
Aromas of berries; tastes of delicate
fruit; delicious and mouthfilling

UMANI RONCHI
1988 Rosso Conero "San Lorenzo"
****   Best-now $7-9**

*A blend of Montepuciano d'Abruzzo
(85%) and Sangiovese (15%); the
essence of delicious Italian wine;
great depth of flavor without an
unpleasant dose of tannin*

VALLOVEREN
1991 Blanc de Noir Robertson Red Muscatel
****   Best-now   8-10**

*Slightly pink; sturdy texture; very
fragrant; tastes of Muscat and spice*

WELLINGTON VINEYARD
1991 Cotes de Sonoma Old Vines
*****   Best-93-98 $8-10**

Stout; mature in taste; round and firm

Riesling

1992

GEYSER PEAK

SOFT JOHANNISBERG RIESLING
NORTH COAST

ALC. 9.8% BY VOL.

The grape and the wine of Alsace. Culti-
vated for centuries along the Rhine river, it has
been spread all over the world. It does not do
well except in the strong sun, producing wine
with a fragrant bouquet that ages well. California produces good wines, but their sweetness
does not have wide appeal in America even
though they are very well made. In California,
if the label says Johannesburg or White
Riesling, it is made from the true German
variety, otherwise, it is probably made from
Sylvaner. In Australia, the wine has soft, floral
scents and can be off-dry or dry. The late
harvest wines are mainly dessert wines here,
but the drier ones will go well with some
lighter pastas, cold poultry, and poached fish.

BASSERMAN-JORDAN *Best Buy*
1989 Kabinett Rheinpfalz
Deideshimer Hohenmorgan
**** Best-now $8-10
Lively, zesty, full-bodied fruit and
pineapple tastes

CHATEAU *Best Buy*
STE. MICHELLE
1990 White Riesling Columbia
Valley Sweet Select
** Best-now $6-8
Flowers and fruit shine through;
uncomplicated and lush

COLUMBIA CREST
1991 Dry Riesling Columbia Valley
** Best-now $7-10
Harmonious, fruity flavors; zesty, soft
and flavorful

DR BURKLIN-WOLF
1991 Kabinett Rheinpfalz
**   Best-now $8-10

*Tart and tasty, but smooth citrus and
fruit scents*

DR BURKLIN-WOLF
1989 Kabinett Rheinpfalz
Wachenheimer Gerumpel
**   Best-now $8-10

*Focused fruit and spice in a wine
sweeter than ordinary*

FRIEDREICH-WILHELM-GYMNASIUM
1991 Qualitatswein Mosel-Saar-Ruwer Falkeunsteiner Hofberg
**   Best - Now $8-10

*Delicate fruit scents and flavors; dry
at the end*

GEYSER PEAK
1992 Soft Johannisberg Riesling
North Coast
***   Best - now $5-7
*Plenty of fruit and spice; brisk and
flavorful*

J & H SELBACH
1991 Qualitatswein Mosel-Saar-
Ruwer Bereich Bernkastel
**   Best - now $5-7
*Uncomplicated; refreshing fruit and
flower scents and tastes*

J & H SELBACH
1991 Qualitatswein Mosel-Saar-
Ruwer Piesporter Michelsberg
**   Best - now $5-9
*Apple and peach scents and tastes;
zesty, light*

KENDALL-JACKSON
1991 Johannisberg Riesling
California Vintner's Reserve
**   Best - now   8-10
*Nice fruitiness start to finish;
uncomplicated*

NAVARRO
1991 Anderson Valley
***   Best-now $8-10
*Voluptuous fruit and honey tastes;
zippy, sweet enough for dessert.*

SELBACH-OSTER
1989 Riesling Hochgewachs Mosel-
Saar-Ruwer Germany
**   Best - now $7-10
Light and refreshing; super apertif

WEGELER-DEINHARD
1989 Kabinett Rheinpfalz
Deidesheimer Herrgottsacker
**   Best-now   9-11
*Harmonious exotic fruits in a medium
dry wine*

WEINGUT GRAFSCHAFT LEININGEN

1990 Kabinett Rheinpfalz Kirchheimer Schwarzerde
**** **Best-now** **$8-10**
Luscious, fresh; citrus and fruit all the way

WEINGUT HALBTROCKEN

1991 Hochgewachs Haltrocken Mosel-Saar-Ruwer Zeltinger Himmelreich
** **Best-now** **$8-10**
Lively finish starts with fruity and flowery scents and flavors

WILLIAM HILL

1989 Williamette Valley Dry White Riesling
*** **Best-now** **$7-9**
Mineral flavors; round, sprightly, crisp

Sauvignon Blanc/
Fumé Blanc

The Sauvignon Blanc is the grape of the White Bordeaux in France. Now Chile, the United States, Australia, and Argentina are all producing good wines from this grape. The style of the wines vary from vintner to vintner and also from year to year. Many are now being fermented and aged in oak. The wines are usually made of only the single grape. They are usually off-dry, brisk, with scents of citrus or fig. Fumé Blanc is used interchangeably with Sauvignon Blanc. The winery itself can choose to use one or both. The Australian and California vintners seem to favor the Fumé Blanc name, but the name itself gives no clue as to the style of the wine. Serve with chicken, boiled shrimp, onion pie, or fish.

CHATEAU   *BEST BUY*
STE MICHELLE
   1990 Columbia Valley
   ***   **Best-now**   **$6-8**
   Fresh, clean, crisp aroma of peach,
   apple, lemon and honey; plenty of
   acidity; flavors of lime and classic
   grassiness; long finish

ESTANCIA   *BEST BUY*
   1990 Monterey
   ****   **Best-now**   **$6-9**
   Full-bodied, figgy, oaky flavors;
   complex

MONTEREY VINEYARD *BEST BUY*
   1991 Classic
   ***   **Best-now**   **$5-7**
   Clean, brisk; good floral aromas;
   refreshing

SILVERADO   *BEST BUY*
1990 Napa Valley
**   Best-now $6-8
Clean and refreshing as any in California; bursting with bright, crisp flavors

ALDERBROOK
1991 Dry Creek
***   Best - 93-95 $7-9
Fruity, brisk, tart, well crafted; mouthfilling

ALDERBROOK
1990 Dry Creek Valley
**   Best-now $7-9
Good fruit and herb tastes; brisk and uncomplicated

ARBOR CREST
1990 Columbia Valley
***   Best-now $6-9
Peachy, clean, and tangy; a touch of spice

ARBORCREST
1990 Columbia Valley
***   Best-93-95 $9-11

Lush and fruity; silky and dry

BEAULIEU VINEYARD
1990 Napa Valley
***   Best-now $8-10

Floral, melony aromas dominate; round, balanced, fresh

BERINGER
1990 Knights Valley Proprietor Grown
***   Best-now $9-11

Harmony with flavorful fruit and oak; lush and mature

BYRON
1991 Santa Barbara County
***   Best-now $8-10

Good fruit and oak make a good blend in a medium bodied wine

CANEPA
1992 Maipo Valley
*** Best-now $4-6
Distinctive citrus and herbal tastes;
uncomplicated; flavorful

CANEPO
1992 Maipo Valley
** Best-now $5-7
Spicy, and herbal, not grassy; clean
and simple

CHATEAU SOUVERAIN
1990 Alexander Valley Barrel
Fermented
** Best-now $7-9
Mellow fruit and fig; soft texture

CLOS JEAN
1992 Sauvignon Bordeaux
*** Best-now $7-9
Aromatic herb and melon scents;
tasty fruit; this is Sauvignon in the
French manner; dry

CONCANNON
1990 Estate Bottled Livermore Valley
***   Best-now $7-9

Peach and apricot aromas and tastes, plus lemon and flowers; clean aftertaste

COOPERS CREEK
1991 Marlborough
**   Best-now $9-11

Focused pepper and citrus aromas and tastes; brisk

COUSINO-MACUL
1992 Maipo
**   Best-now $5-7

Essence of cinnamon perks up fruit tastes; brisk, clean, and even

DOMAINE DE L'ARJOLLE
1992 Vin du Pays Cotes de Thongues
***   Best-now $6-8

Just an essence of herb and melon; light and fruity; clean and brisk

DOMAINE DES ACACIAS
1992   Sauvignon Touraine
***   **Best-now $6-8**
Flavorful fruit and spice; truffle or earthy aromas; delicate body

DOMAINE LA COLUMBETTE
1991 Vin du Pays
Coteaux du Livron
***   **Best-93-94 $9-11**
Focused herb and spice aromas; opulent fruit flavors; robust finish

DOMAINE RABAT
1992 Maipo Valley
**   **Best-now $4-6**
Lush citrus and fruit aromas and flavors; a touch of grass on the finish

GEYSER PEAK
1992   Sonoma
***   **Best-now $6-8**
Brisk and elegant; flowers, fruit, and melon scents and tastes

GUENOC
1990 Estate Bottled Guenoc Valley
*** Best-now $9-11

Oaky, grassy bouquet; velvety in the mouth with wood and citrus impressions; clean dry lemony finish

HOGUE WASHINGTON
1991 Fumé Blanc
*** Best-now $5-7

Smoky, floral, fresh-mouth feel; melony

HUSCH
1991 Mendocino
*** Best-now $8-10

Brisk, flowery; lots of fruit; delicate

IVAN TAMAS
1991 Livermore
*** Best-now $6-8

Focused melon, honey, and herbs; mouthfilling, flavorful

JOULLIAN VINEYARDS
1990 Carmel Valley
**   Best-now $6-8

Crisp with citrus and fig notes; bright and clean

KENDALL-JACKSON
1991 California Vintner's Reserve
**   Best-now $8-10

An uncomplicated, fruity wine; delicate

LAMBERT BRIDGE
1990 Fumé Blanc Sonoma County
***   Best-now $9-11

Concentrated herb and fruit, lively and tasty

MURPHY-GOODE
1991 Alexander Valley
**   Best-now $7-9

Pleasant, muscat-like spiciness not characteristic of a Fumé Blanc

NAUTILUS
1991 Hawkes Bay, New Zealand
*** Best-now $8-10

*Aromatic melon and herbal scents;
spicy fruit flavors; brisk and flavorful*

PEDRONCELLI
1991 Dry Creek Valley
*** Best-now $6-8

*Nice fruit, mineral and herb aromas
and flavors*

PETER LEHMANN
1988 Barossa Valley
*** Best-93-95 $8-10

*Rich, agreeable mint, spice and
pepper; soft, flavorful*

PETER LEHMANN
1990 Barossa Valley
*** Best-94-96 $8-10

*Sturdy fruit and pepper scents and
tastes; easy to drink*

PRESTON VINEYARDS
1991 Cuvee de Fumé Dry Creek
***   Best-now $9-11

Brisk and rich; focused honey, melon, and fig aromas

ROO'S LEAP
1991 Fumé Blanc Barossa Valley
**   Best-now $7-9

Clean, zesty, citrusy and tangy; harmonious

SANTA RITA
1991 Maipo Valley "120" Series
***   Best-now $4-6

Fresh herbal scents and taste; oak lends depth

STONELEIGH
1991 Marlborough
*** **Best-now** **$7-9**
Luscious; mature fruit and herbs blend well

STRATFORD
1991 Partner's Reserve California
*** **Best-now** **$8-10**
Delicious fruit and herb aromas; agreeable tastes and acidity

WILDHURST
1991 Clear Lake
*** **Best-now** **$8-10**
Brisk citrus and herb aromas and flavors; fresh on the finish

Semillon

The grape of the fabulous Chateau d'Yquem at several hundred dollars per bottle, and also Sauternes, Australia has done more with the Semillon, where it is very popular. There it is mainly produced as a single varietal where it has lots of oak and is full-bodied and rich. In France and the U.S., the Semillon is blended with Sauvignon Blanc or Chardonnay. There wines are usually off-dry, with some sweetness. They can age for up to seven years or more. Try the sweeter Sauternes with dessert. The dryer wines will go well served cold with cream soups, and light fare.

COLUMBIA CREST *BEST BUY*
1991 Columbia Valley Semillon Chardonnay
** **Best-now** **$5-7**
Some apple, lots of fig; uncomplicated and crisp

LINDEMANS *BEST BUY*
1991 Semillon Chardonnay South Eastern Australia Bin 77
*** **Best-now** **$6-8**
Uncomplicated; crisp fig and vanilla scents; zesty on the finish

CLOS DU VAL
1989 Semillon Stags Leap District
*** **Best-now** **$9-11**
Nicely focused citrus and vanilla; delicious

COLDRIDGE
1992 South Eastern Australia
***   Best-now $5-7
Zesty, clean, good fruit;
uncomplicated

COSENTINO
1990 Semillon Napa Valley
***   Best-now $8-11
Tobacco, fruit, and citrus joined in a
mellow blend

GEYSER PEAK
1991 Semchard California
**** Best-94-96 $8-10
Concentrated smoke and citrus scents
and tastes; full-bodied

GEYSER PEAK
1992 Semchard Monterey
***   Best-now $6-8
Mouthfilling; zesty; good fruit and
spice scents and tastes

JOSEPH SWAN
1990 Semillon Sonoma Mountain Berlin
**   **Best-now** $7-9

Mature, liberal toast and fruit; a little tart

LINDEMANS
1990 Semillon Chardonnay South Eastern Australia Bin 77
**   **Best-now** $5-7

Replete with flavors; delicate pear and melon scents

ROSEMOUNT
1992 Semillon Chardonnay Australia
***   **Best-now** $8-10

Clean, good fruit and honey; brisk finish

SEPPELT
1991 Semillon Chardonnay South Australia Moyston
**   **Best-now** $6-8

Delicate smoothness; mellow citrus and fruit flavor

Shiraz/Rhone

In the third century, the Roman Emperor, Probus, made it mandatory to plant the Syrah vine on the hills of the Rhone Valley; here the great L'Hermitage is made. California has some plantings, and Australia has planted large acreages. There they have developed sturdy wines, high in alcohol, but most are now full-bodied with lots of cassis and blackberry flavors. California is producing very limited quantities. Australia is producing larger quantities of very good Shiraz. Serve with the milder cheeses, grilled fish, and roasted foul.

ASHWOOD *Best Buy*

1991 River Willow Australia
***   Best-95-97 $6-8
Full-bodied; lush oak, fruit and
cherry; good oak finish; 80% Shiraz

GEORGES DUBOEUF *Best Buy*

1991 Cotes de Rhone Domaine des
Moulins
**** Best-94-02 $5-7
Concentrated and opulent; mature
fruit and great tannins

GEORGES DUBOEUF *Best Buy*

1992   Syrah Rose Vin du Pays
d'Oc
***   Best-now $4-6
A full-bodied rose; fragrant, clean,
and fruity

HARDY'S *Best Buy*
1991 Shiraz-Cabernet South Eastern Australia Captain's Selection
*** **Best-now** $5-7

Balanced cherry and fruit, spice and chocolate at the finish

LA VIEILLE FERME *Best Buy*
1991 Cotes du Luberon Rhone White
*** **Best-now** $5-7

Fresh melony flavors; light body; refreshing

LA VIELLE FERME *Best Buy*
1990 Cotes du Rhone Blanc Gold Label
*** **Best-now** $7-9

Luscious fruit and honey scents and tastes; full-bodied

ROSEMOUNT   *BEST BUY*
1991 South Eastern Australia
***   Best-now $7-10
Concentrated cherry, spice, and
vanilla; firm texture

TYRRELL'S   *BEST BUY*
1991 Long Flat Red South Eastern
Australia
**   Best-now $6-8
Silky, flavorful; nice cherry and fruit;
delightful

WYNDHAM   *BEST BUY*
1990 South Eastern Australia Bin
555
***   Best-now $6-8
Mature berry and fruit along with
spice; flavorful

ANDREW GARRETT
1991 Australia Bols Style
***   Best-now $8-10
Spice, berry, chocolate; full-bodied;
luscious

ANDREW GARRETT
1991   McLaren's Red Australia
**   Best-now $6-8
*Mellow spice and berry; sound
tannin; refreshing*

ARROWFIELD
1991 Shiraz-Cabernet Australia
**   Best-93-97 $9-11
*Mature, clean; focused cherry,
vanilla, and chocolate*

ARUNDA
1991 Shiraz-Cabernet
Southeastern Australia
**   Best-now $5-7
*Easy to drink; fruity with some
pepper and cherry scents and tastes*

ASHWOOD
1991 Riverland
***   Best-now $8-10
*Zesty; silky with fruit and smoke; lots
of gusto*

ASTIER

1991 Cotes du Rhone
**   Best-now $4-6
Peppery scents; fruity, light; balanced

BLACK OPAL

1990 South Eastern Australia
**   Best-94-96 $7-9
Firm; good berry and fruit scents and tastes along with lots of tannin

BROWN BROTHERS

1990 Victoria Family Selection
***   Best-now $8-10
Tangy, uncomplicated; silky-berry tastes

CHAEAU DE VALLONIERES

1990   Cotes du Rhone
***   Best-now $8-10
Silky peppers and fruit tastes; medium body; flavorful

CHATEAU DES TOURS
1989 Reserve Cotes du Rhone
** Best-now $8-10

Pepper and earthy flavors of a more costly Chateauneuf du Pape

CLOS DE LA MURE
1990 Cotes du Rhone
*** Best-93-95 $8-10

Generous nose of spice, cherries and fruit; flavorful and penetrating on the finish

COLDRIDGE
1992 Shiraz-Cabernet South Eastern Australia
** Best-now $5-7

Soft, smooth, moderate amounts of cherry and spice scents and tastes

COLDRIDGE
1992 South Eastern Australia
***   **Best-now** $5-7

Voluptuous; loaded with berry and pepper; supple finish

COLUMBIA CREST
1990 Columbia Valley
***   **Best-93-96** $9-11

Robust and soft, herbs, currants, and oak; firm and concentrated

CRANSWICK
1990 Shiraz-Merlot South Eastern Australia
**   **Best-now** $6-8

Brisk, uncomplicated; dark cherry flavor

CRANSWICK ESTATE
1990 Shiraz-Cabernet South Eastern Australia
**   Best-now $6-8

Zesty, mature; good oak and tannin with cherry notes

CUVEE KERMIT LYNCH
1990 Cotes du Rhone
***   Best-93-97 $6-9

Mature fruit; mellow spice; delightful pepper and fruit flavors

D'ARENBERG
1989 McLaren Valley Old Vine
***   Best-95-97 $7-9

Mellow, harmonious blend of cherry, fruit and tobacco; full-bodied

DANIEL COMBE
1990 Vignoble de la Jasse-Cote du Rhone
***   Best-93-96 $8-10

Exhuberant, delicate, yet loaded with fruit, mouthfilling

DAVID WYNN
1992 South Eastern Australia
***   Best-now $9-11
Fresh, silky; good fruit, pepper, and cassis; mellow finish

DOMAINE ANDRE BRUSSET
1991 Cuvee Sommelongues-Dorees-Tradition
***   Best-93-95 $7-9
Berry, cherry, and spice aromas; saturated flavors; mature and fresh

DOMAINE BRUSSET
1991 Cairanne Cotes du Rhone
***   Best-93-96 $8-10
Plentiful pepper, berry, and truffle aromas; lush, mature; smooth fruit tastes

DOMAINE DE BEAUMALRIC
1992 Cotes du Rhone
***   Best-now $8-10
Scents of exotic fruit, flowers and honey; brisk and agreeable

DOMAINE DE BEAURENARD
1990 Cotes du Rhone
***   Best-94-97 $8-10

Herbs and ripe fruit aromas and flavors; complex and generous; good tannins

DOMAINE DES ARMOURIERS
1992 Cotes du Rhone
***   Best-93-95 $6-8

Mouthfilling spice, pepper, and fruit; luscious

DOMAINE DES MOULINS
1990 Cotes du Rhone
Georges Dubœuf
**   Best-now $4-6

A dark, ruby-colored wine with a big, rich cherry style

DOMAINE LA COLUMBETTE
1990 Vin du Pays
Coteaux du Livron
*** Best-93-96 $9-11
Scents of cassis, smoke, and mint;
agreeable tannins; full-bodied

DUBOEUF
1990 Cotes du Rhone
Aires Veilles Estate
** Best-now $5-8
Deep, peppery, grapey flavors; soft

GRANT SMITH
1990 Riverina Valley Shiraz/
Cabernet Bin 95
*** Best-now $6-8
Syrah pepperiness; fruity, soft, well-
balanced

HAWTHORN HILL
1990 South Eastern Australia Bin 5000
***   **Best-now $6-8**

Mature berry and fruit along with spice; flavorful

HOUGHTON
1990 Western Australia Wildflower Ridge
***   **Best-95-97 $8-10**

Loaded with berry and cherry scents and tastes; toasty oak overtones

JAMIESON'S RUN
1990 Shiraz-Cabernet Coonawarra
****   **Best-93-96 $9-11**

Graceful, zesty; smooth berry, fruit, and herb scents and tastes

LA VIELLE FERME
1990 Cotes du Rhone Gold Label Rhone White
***   **Best-now $7-9**

Intense spice and berry aromas; silky tannins; hearty and flavorful

LA VIELLE FERME
1990 Cotes du Rhone Reserve
***   Best-93-97 $7-9
Graceful spice scents; generous fruit and cherry tastes; easy to drink

LA VIELLE FERME
1991 Cotes du Rhone Reserve
**   Best-now $7-9
Lean spice and fig flavors; harmonious, flavorful

LA VIELLE FERME
1990 Cotes du Ventoux
***   Best-now $7-9
Soft and full of fruit, essence of herb and cassis; opulent

MCGUIGAN BROTHERS
1991 South Eastern Australia Black
**   Best-94-96 $6-8
Delightful texture; good oak and dark sugar; wait on tannins to subside

MICHELTON
1991 Victoria
***   Best-93-95 $9-11
Essence of cassis; luscious mature fruit; mouthfilling

MITCHELTON
1991 Riverland
**   Best-now $8-10
Generous berry, fruit, and spice; brisk

MITCHELTON
1990 Victoria
***   Best-now $7-9
Focused and silky; mellow fruit and berry tastes; oak and spice notes

PENFOLDS
1990 Shiraz-Cabernet South Australia Koonunga Hill
***   Best-95-97 $8-10
Rich, hearty, focused berry and fruit scents; one-third Cabernet

ROSEMOUNT
1991 Australia
***   Best-93-95   9-11
*Mellow cassis and pepper aromas;
silky texture; flavorful*

ROSEMOUNT
1992 Shiraz Cabernet Australia
***   Best-now $8-10
*Fragrant cassis and pepper aromas;
silky texture; flavorful*

RYECROFT
1992 McLaren Vale Flame Tree
****   Best-93-96 $7-9
*Nicely balanced berry and cherry
scents and tastes; uncomplicated*

SEPPELT
1989 South Australia Black Label
***   Best-now $9-11
*Concentrated berry, spice and cherry
scents and tastes; slightly dry*

SEPPELT
1989 South Eastern Australia Reserve Bin
*** **Best-94-96 $8-10**
Brisk and fresh; plenty of fruit and good tannins

WYNDHAM
1990 Shiraz South Eastern Australia Bin 555
** **Best-now $6-9**
Supple, harmonious essence of fruit and citrus

WYNDHAM
1988 South Eastern Australia Bin 555
** **Best-now $6-8**
Modest fruit and citrus; mellow, flavorful

YALUMBA
1989 Barossa Valley Family Reserve
*** **Best-now $8-10**
Very sturdy, cherry and currant scents and tastes; strong and flavorful

Sparkling Wines

ANNA DE CODORNIU

CODORNIU
1551

RAVENTOS
1872

Codorníu

BRUT

CAVA
SPARKLING WINE

MÉTHODE TRADITIONNELLE - MÉTHODE CHAMPENOISE
ELABORADOR CODORNIU, S.A. SANT SADURNÍ D'ANOIA-ESPAÑA
PRODUCT OF SPAIN   Fermented in this bottle

750 ML.
Alc.11.5% by vol.

If it is made in the Champagne District of France, under their strict regulations, then it is Champagne. If it is made anywhere else, even in France, then it must be labeled "sparkling" wine. Other than charging the bottle with carbon dioxide, there are two methods of making sparkling wines. The "Natural Method" uses only the natural sugars in the grapes to carry out the first and second fermentations. It is the second fermentation which produces the bubbles. The "Method Champenoise" uses other sugars to aid in the first fermentation; the second fermentation takes place after liqueur and cane sugar are added before the bottles are filled. Brut sparkling wine is the driest, followed by Extra Dry and Dry. The Spanish, along with a few California producers, seem to be making much of the lower-priced sparkling wine. This is the celebration wine, the toasting wine; try it with most anything.

DEINHARD   *Best Buy*
NV Brut Lila Vin Mousseux
**   **Best-now**   **$7-9**
Zesty, flowery, brisk finish

DOMAINE STE.   *Best Buy*
MICHELLE
NV Blanc de Blanc
Columbia Valley
***   **Best-now**   **$7-10**
Lots of fruit and spice; dry and harmonious

FREIXENET   *Best Buy*
NV Brut Cordon Negro
**   **Best-now**   **$8-10**
Uncomplicated, light, and fruity

ANDREW GARRETT
NV Australia Cuvee
*** Best-now $9-11

Smooth feel, with lemon tastes

BALLATORE
NV Gran Spumante California
*** Best-now $6-8

Clean and zesty; lots of exotic fruit and spice

CA DEL SOLO
1991 Moscato del Solo Monterey
** Best-now $8-10

Fragrant, zesty; gentle citrus and fruit scents and tastes

CODORNIU
1989 Brut Anna de Codorniu
** Best-now $8-10

Tart; refreshing citrus tastes

CODORNIU
1988 Brut Blanc de Blancs
** Best-now $9-11

Exotic fruit and citrus

CODORNIU
1990 Brut Cava Clasico
** Best-now $6-8

Flavorful, zesty, flowery; uncomplicated

CODORNIU
1990 Brut Clasico
** Best-now $6-8

Zesty, flowery scents; uncomplicated; nice

DOMAINE STE MICHELLE
NV Blanc de Blancs Brut
*** Best-now $8-10

Delicate, brisk; good fruit; good bubbles

DOMAINE STE MICHELLE
NV Brut Washington
***   Best-now $7-10
Light, spicy fruit; brisk, good bubbles

DOMAINE STE. MICHELLE
NV Brut Columbia Valley
**   Best-now $8-10
Fruity, fresh, and a little sweet;
uncomplicated

DUBOSC
NV Brut
**   Best-now $9-11
Stout and sweet with melon taste

LEMBEY
1985 Brut
**   Best-now $8-10
Harmonious blend of fruit and citrus;
uncomplicated

MIRO
NV Brut
** **Best-now** $9-11
Full-bodied and harmonious

PAUL CHENAU
NV Brut Blanc de Blancs Cava
** **Best-now** $8-10
Refreshing; plenty of fruit and flower scents and tastes

ROBERT PECOTA
1992 Mustcato di Andrea
Napa Valley
*** **Best-now** $8-10
Supple, citrus scents and tastes; clean finish

ROTARI
1988 Brut Riserva
** **Best-now** $9-11
Lively, spice and fruit in harmony right to the end

SARDA
    NV Brut
    ** **Best-now** $9-11
    Strong fruit and sweetness

XENIUS
    NV Brut Cava Reserva
    ** **Best-now** $8-10
    Brisk citrus; zesty; very flavorful

White

This group of wines has some pleasant surprises in store for the wine explorer. Well-made, mostly blends, they are very inexpensive and very good. Some are almost experimental blends that appear and disappear over time. Good whites come from all over; Australia, New Zealand, Europe, and California. They should be chilled and, in general, served with lighter fare. A good category to explore.

CHATEAU DE CABRIAC

1989 Corbieres
***   Best-now $5-7
Intense herbal aromas; plummy,
dense

FIRESTONE

BEST BUY

NV Prosperity White
Santa Inez Valley
**   Best-now $4-6
Flowery, light, a little sweet, fruity;
delightful for sipping

MIRASSOU

BEST BUY

1991 Pinot Blanc Monterey County
Fifth Generation Family Selection
***   Best-now $6-8
Lush fruit flavors; harmonious and
dry; delightful

MONTEREY VINEYARDS

BEST BUY

1991 Classic
***   Best-now $3-5
Good fruity aromas and flavors;
clean, brisk

ANDRE-MICHEL BREGON
1991 Muscat
***   Best-now $9-11
Fragrant with lime and spice;
uncomplicated, brisk, and flavorful

BEAUCLAIRE
1990 Vin de Pays des
Cotes de Gascogne
**   Best-now $4-6
Flavorful, delicate, and flowery

BONNY DOON
1991 Ca Del Solo Moscato
***   Best-now $7-9
Flavorful; rich with fruit and pine-
apple; flowery essences

CHATEAU BONNET
1990 Entre Deux Mers
***   Best-now $6-8
Fragrant herb, honey, and floral
scents and flavors; clean soft body

CHATEAU CALABRE
1992 Montravel
*** **Best-now** **$6-8**
Lively spice and herbal aromas and flavors; full-bodied and brisk

CHATEAU DE CAMPUGET
1992 Costiere de Nimes
*** **Best-now** **$5-7**
Aromatic with fruit and flowers; refreshing, clean, medium body

COLDRIDGE
1991 South Eastern Australia
*** **Best-now** **$6-8**
Good fruit aroma and flavor; buttery notes; modest body

COLUMBIA CREST
1990 Columbia Valley
*** **Best-now** **$7-9**
Zesty, fruit, citrus, and spice tastes; lively, clean, and flavorful; a touch of oak at the end

DANIEL GEHRS
1991 Le Chenay Monterey
*** Best-93-95 $6-8
Brisk; honey and flower scents and tastes; flavorful

DOMAINE DE BARRET
1991 Cotes de Gascogne Reserve
*** Best-now $8-10
Subtle aromas of flowers, cherry and spice; lots of fruit, delicious

ELLISTON
1991 Pinot Blanc Central Coast Sunol Valley Vineyard
** Best-now $9-11
Smooth, mature fruit tastes; uncomplicated and tasty

GEORGES DUBOEUF
1992 Chazan Vin du Pays d'OC
*** Best-now $4-6
Aromatic, flowery aromas; agreeable fruit; tart

GEORGES DUBOEUF
1992 Saint-Veran
Domaine St.-Martin
***   Best-now $7-9
*Fragrant and fruity; concentrated
honey and floral aromas*

HARDY'S
1991 South Eastern Australia
Captain's Selection
**   Best-now $5-7
Harmonious, but a little rigid

IVAN TAMAS
1991 Trebbiano Livermore
***   Best-now $8-10
Lots of fruit; luscious, rich

LA VIELLE FERME
1990 Cotes du Luberon
***   Best-now $7-9
Essence of flowers; brisk and tart

LAURENT CHARLES BROTTE
1991 Vioguier Vin de Pays d'Oc
** Best-now $7-9
Fragrant and flavorful example of Viognier; focused

MAITRE D'ESTOURNEL
1990 Bordeaux Blanc
*** Best-now $8-10
Old white bordeaux style; almondy

MICHELTON
1992 Marsanne Goulburn
*** Best-now $9-11
Aromas of fruit, melon, and honey; tangy fruit; nice acidity, brisk

MITCHELTON
1991 Marsanne Goulburn Valley
*** Best-now $7-9
Full-bodied, tasty; scents of honey and pear

MITCHELTON
1991 Semillon
Chardonnay Victoria
** **Best-now** **$7-9**
Plain, tasty, and zesty; refreshing

MONTE VOLPE
1991 Moscato Mendocino
** **Best-now** **$7-9**
Harmonious fruit and spice; very sweet and clean

NAVARRO
1990 Edelzwicker Mendocino
*** **Best-now** **$6-8**
Clean, brisk; lots of fruit and spice scents and tastes; a little sweet

PIERRE BONEFACE
1992 Apremont Les Rocailles
*** **Best-now** **$7-9**
Loaded with fruit; dry and clean; brisk and a little fizzy

RABBIT RIDGE
1991 Mystique, Proprietary White Sonoma Valley
***   **Best-now**   **$8-10**
Good fruit; fresh, brisk, delightful

RESPLANDY
1990 Marsanne Vin de Pays d'Oc
**   **Best-now**   **$7-9**
Gentle and even scents of flowers and fruit

ROBERT PECOTA
1991 Mucato di Andres Napa Valley
**   **Best-now**   **$8-11**
Just right sweetness; spice and melon scents and tastes

ROBERT PECOTA
1991 Muscat Napa Valley Muscato de Andrea
**   **Best-now**   **$9-11**
Concentrated, fruity, and slightly sweet; harmonious and clean

TENUTA VILANOVA
1990 Pinot Grigio Italy
**   Best-now $8-10
Full-bodied, clean, with depth of flavor

TRIMBACH
1989 Pinot Blanc d'Alsace
**   Best-now $8-10
Crisp, juicy, full-bodied; versatile with a wide variety of foods

VANLOVEREN
1991 Pinot Gris Robertson
***   Best-now $9-10
Honey, vanilla, and fruit; creamy texture; luscious

WEINGUT GRAFSCHAFT LEININGEN
1989 Rulander Auslese Halbtrocken Rheinpfalz Kirchheimer Romerstrabe Renominee
**   Best-now $9-11
Tart; drier than most; fairly rough

Zinfandel

The vine seems to be unique to California, where it has been planted since the 1800's. So far, no one has been able to trace it back to Europe or to any other continent. California has five climate zones, and this adaptable grape grows well in all of them. The "blush" wines are made of Zinfandel, but the real thing is entirely different. These are off-dry and easy to drink. Consumers are realizing that the best of the Zinfandels come from the Napa and Sonoma valleys. Here, the wines are outstanding. These are rich, full-bodied, and very fruity. They have a ruby color, and flavors of berries and peppers. These are good outdoor wine, complimenting barbecued fowl and red meats.

CANTERBURY *BEST BUY*
1990 California
*** **Best-now** **$4-6**
Silky and flavorful; zesty scents;
blackberry essence

ERNEST & JULIO *BEST BUY*
GALLO
1987 Sonoma
*** **Best-now** **$4-6**
Lush fruit; full body; clean and fresh

MEEKER *BEST BUY*
1990 Dry Creek Valley
Gold Leaf Cuvee
**** **Best-93-97** **$9-11**
Concentrated berry and cherry and
fruit tastes; a harmonious blend

MONTEVINA *BEST BUY*
1990 Amador County Brioso
*** **Best-now** **$6-9**
Fresh, zesty; lots of berry taste; even
and delicate

RAVENSWOOD *BEST BUY*
1989 North Coast Zinfandel
Vintner's Blend
***** Best-now $8-10
Peppery berry flavors; complex
aromas; truly luscious

BARON HERZOG
1990 Sonoma County
Special Cuvee
*** Best-now $9-11
Fragrant fruit and berry essences
blend well with tannins

BOEGER
1990 El Dorado Walker Vineyard
***** Best-now $9-11
Luscious, silky, mellow blend of
currant and plum

BUEHLER
1990 Napa Valley
*** Best-now $8-10
Rich scents and flavors of berries,
raisins, chocolate; balanced

FRANCISCAN
1990 Napa Valley
**** Best-now $9-11
*Complex black currant, pepper, and
spices; fruity/floral, intense*

MANZANITA RIDGE
1988 Alexander Valley
*** Best-93-95 $7-9
Focused; berry scents and taste

MARTIN BROTHERS
1990 Paso Robles Primitivo
** Best-93-95 $8-10
*Berry tastes in an uncomplicated,
refreshing Zinfandel*

ORGANIC WINE WORKS
1992 Napa County
** Best-now $9-11
*Full-bodied; mature; berry and fruit
but lots of grape flavor*

RABBIT RIDGE
1991 Dry Creek Valley
***   **Best-93-96   \$9-11**
Lots of tannin; plenty of fruit; firm texture; give it time

RAVENSWOOD
1991 North Coast Vintner's Blend
***   **Best-now   \$6-9**
Good fruit, strong spice; mouthfilling

RIDGE PASO ROBLES
1990 Zinfandel
****   **Best-now   \$9-11**
Peppery, oaky; intense, complex tannins; soft

ROSENBLUM
NV California Cuvee VI
****   **Best-now   \$8-10**
Very big fruit flavors, especially raspberry; excellent acid; youthfully tannic

ROSENBLUM
NV California Vintner's Cuvee V
** Best-now $6-8
Mellow berry and pepper scents and tastes; uncomplicated

ROUND HILL
1990 Napa Valley
*** Best-93-96 $5-7
Fruit and spice balance off heavy oak; refreshing

SANTA BARBARA
1992 Santa Inez Valley Beaujour
** Best-now $7-10
Fresh and flavorful

SEBASTIANI
1988 Sonoma County
**** Best-now $6-8
Concentrated cherry, blackberry flavors; fragrant, spicy

SEGESIO
1990 Sonoma County
***   Best-93-96 $6-8
Concentrated, intense berry and spice and vanilla; approaches elegance

STRATFORD
1991 California
***   Best-93-96 $9-11
Berry and pepper aromas; spicy, tasty

SUTTER HOME
1989 Amador Reserve
****   Best-now $9-11
Ripe plum flavors; brawny, heavy texture

TRENTADUE
1990 Sonoma
***   Best-93-98 $9-11
Lithe, firm cherry scents and tastes; luscious

TRENTADUE
1991 Sonoma
**** Best-93-01 $9-11
*Mellow spice scents and tastes; bold
and mouthfilling*

VALLEY RIDGE
1988 Sonoma
** Best-now $6-8
*Intense raspberry fruit; smooth,
delicate texture; very appealing*

WILDHURST
1990 Clear Lake
*** Best-now $6-8
*Crisp and fragrant; rich with berry
scent and taste*